ON
WATCHING
BIRDS

ON
WATCHING
BIRDS

By
LAWRENCE KILHAM

Illustrations by
JOAN WALTERMIRE
Foreword by
JOHN K. TERRES

CHELSEA GREEN
PUBLISHING COMPANY
Chelsea, Vermont

Library of Congress Cataloging-in-Publication Data

    On watching birds / by Lawrence Kilham.
      p.   cm.
    Bibliography: p.
    Includes index.
    ISBN 0-930031-14-8 (alk. paper): $17.95
    1. Wildlife watching—Technique, 2. Birds—Behavior—Study and
teaching. 3. Bird watching—Technique. I. Title.
QL60.K55 1988
598'.07'234—dc19   88-2060
                                            CIP

*To my wife Jane, whose aid and companionship
added much to the success of our
watchings*

ACKNOWLEDGMENTS

The observations making up this book are in part hitherto un-published and in part abstracted and written in a more general style from among 190 notes and articles that I have published in *The Auk*, *Wilson Bulletin*, *Condor*, *Journal of Field Ornithology*, *Florida Field Naturalist*, *Oriole*, *Canadian Field-Naturalist*, *American Midland Naturalist*, and *Journal of Mammalogy*. I am obliged to Eldon D. Greij for permission to reprint observations on "Pileated Pairing" from *Birder's World*.

My three previous books, *Never Enough of Nature* (1977, re-published by Stackpole in 1981 as *A Naturalist's Field Guide*); *Life Histories of the Woodpeckers of Eastern North America*; and *The American Crow and the Common Raven* (scheduled to appear in January 1989, from Texas A & M University Press) have pro-vided additional background.

CONTENTS

FOREWORD

In introducing Dr. Kilham to the readers of this book, I do not want to keep him offstage any longer than it takes to tell what a remarkably close observer he is. It may or may not be unusual that a medical man who has spent years studying viruses should also be a fine naturalist, but I think there is a correlation. As a medical researcher, Dr. Kilham must be an acute observer, and I am deeply impressed with his clear descriptions and with the details he notes of all that he sees, hears, feels, and senses.

I have kept a naturalist's journal of my own observations for more than fifty years, and I know the excitement of watching wildlife—birds, especially—that Dr. Kilham brings to us in his book. He has done this extraordinarily well, not only because he is a good writer, but because of his love and respect for his subjects and his contagious enthusiasm, which brightens every page. His methods of observing, and his keen analysis of what he has seen and felt, will, I think, open a door for each of us, possibly to a familiar marsh, pond, forest, or river bank so that we may see it as we have not seen it before.

Curiosity is Dr. Kilham's driving force. Curiosity spurs a naturalist in his endless search to know more and more about a bird or any other wild animal, to learn perhaps only a little about it in the beginning, but to pick up at every opportunity where one has left off.

Whenever Dr. Kilham took a walk or went anywhere, he tells us he started watching the first birds he met. "Watch everything," he writes. His system of behavior watching worked so well that he could always come home with something learned, something to write about in his notes. No matter how many experts might have reported the behavior of such common birds as Blue Jays and chickadees, Dr. Kilham decided to "see and discover everything for myself." He followed his observations by reading what others had discovered about each bird or other animal he had watched. This helped him to learn what was known or unknown about each and made him a more informed observer next time he followed up his earlier observations.

His equipment is simple: a pair of binoculars, a pen and paper for note taking (the *sine qua non* of being a good observer), and an easy-to-carry folding chair. Being comfortable while watching, whether one is old or young, makes the observer contented to stay in one place and to watch even when little is happening.

Thoreau, by Walden Pond, wrote: "You need only sit still long enough in some attractive spot in the woods that all its inhabitants may exhibit themselves to you."

Dr. Kilham's subjects in behavior watching are astonishingly varied. We know that he must have studied, at one time, every bird, mammal, or insect that he met or that interested him. From warblers and sparrows, to hawks, owls, grebes, herons, Anhingas, and Wild Turkeys; from hornbills in Africa (a splendid study), guans, Orange-breasted Falcons in Guatemala, and the small rabbitlike pikas of the Rockies (a major study), to whirligig beetles on quiet ponds—nothing escapes his close attention, his eager, persistent pursuit. The author's studies of crow behavior, of woodpeckers, especially the Pileated and Red-headed, are fascinating, highly important contributions to our knowledge of these birds.

Animal watching, behavior watching, or simply bird watching, must have begun thousands of years ago among certain men and women because of their interest in wild animals and their love or simple affection for them. The German philosopher Schopenhauer had words for such feelings when he wrote:

> The sight of any free animal going about its business undisturbed, seeking its food, or looking after its young, or mixing in the company of its kind, all the time being exactly what it ought to be, and can be—what a strange pleasure it gives us.

But something more must be added if we, like Dr. Kilham, are to know the fulfillment that comes with one's own discoveries, often chance discoveries that lead us to others of even greater significance.

"Behavior watching is cumulative," Dr. Kilham advises, "and when one gets the knack of it, the more one sees and reflects, the more one is apt to observe. And reading, creative reading of the kind that generates ideas and sparks enthusiasm, can be a great asset if you want to keep right on through old age."

There are many professional books about studies of animal behavior, but most are written by scientists for scientists. Dr. Kilham has written a book for bird watchers, about the joys of watching, how to go about it, and how to make one's observations meaningful. And perhaps best of all, Dr. Kilham has written a first-rate autobiography, one that brings us a life filled with accomplishments.

I have found an affirmation of Dr. Kilham's work, written more than a hundred years ago by Dr. Elliott Coues, one of America's greatest ornithologists. Coues was a naturalist, an effective public speaker, and a brilliant and prolific writer whose popularizing of ornithology was the most effective of his time.

For myself, [he wrote], the time is past, happily or not, when every bird was an agreeable surprise, for dewdrops do not last all day; but I have never walked in the woods without learning something that I did not know before. . . . How can you, with so much before you, keep out of the woods another minute?

John K. Terres
New Canaan, Connecticut
February 1988

PREFACE

*There are many kinds of study. Those whose studies
are of the real and rare kind get the habit. They
can't throw it off. It is too good and they go on
studying the rest of their lives.*

Robert Henri

A publisher once suggested to me that I write a how-to book on
studying bird behavior. I realized the project would be impossible, even though I have spent many thousands of hours watching
the behavior of many kinds of birds, some mammals, and a few
reptiles. There are too many individual ways of watching wildlife. Some people will prefer one, some another. You can write a
book on how to identify birds, or how to attract birds, but a book
on how to study behavior would necessarily be an oversimplifica-
tion. One watcher will have one kind of background, and another will have a different one, and this very diversity can be of
value in learning about even the commonest birds. Every bird is
a miracle. A variety of approaches to birds' behavior, I think,
will tell us more than any single method that is standardized.

What I seek in this book, therefore, is not to hand beginners
cut flowers but to give them tips on growing their own; not to
provide accounts applicable to only a few birds, but to give
pointers on how to go about observing almost any bird anywhere, as well as some mammals and reptiles. In attempting to
do this I use my own experience primarily. I would be glad to
draw more on the experiences of others, but it is difficult, in
reading notes or articles in journals, to understand how others
have gone about making their observations and why they have
made the observations they have.

This book arose from a seminar on watching bird behavior
that I gave at the Montshire Museum in Hanover, New Hampshire. Finding that I could talk better about things I knew at first
hand, I arranged my teaching material much as in this book. I

did not try to tell everything but simply to abstract pertinent points from my own observations, some of which I have published in the course of the last forty years.

There are many today who would enjoy watching birds and animals systematically if they had some idea of how to go about doing so. Studying behavior is not, of course, the only way of being interested in birds. Monumental are the numbers of birders who, according to a recent issue of *Time*, are dedicated to competitive listing of the species they have seen and traveling to "hot spots" where rarities can be found. An attraction of this kind of birding, aside from its competitiveness, is its companionability. As one enthusiast quoted by *Time* exclaimed, "Camaraderie is what birding is all about."

The opposite approach is that of the professional ornithologist. Although one can make no easy generalizations, the trend among professionals interested in bird behavior is to write articles so studded with graphs, charts, and statistics that little remains having to do with whole, living birds. Many professionals seem to regard making broad generalizations as their goal. But, as E. O. Wilson has pointed out, "The race to make discoveries of the greatest generality, to solve the major problems in the 'mainstream of biology,' does not strike me as the best research strategy to teach to students. It results in an implosive convergence of effort on a few subjects, in a sharp decline in the number of discoveries per man per unit time, and in frustration on the part of young scientists who realize too late that their own professors have picked up the best pebbles on the beach."

Donald R. Griffin also has reservations about scientific studies of behavior. In his book *Animal Thinking* he repeatedly makes the point that "Most biologists and psychologists tend, explicitly or implicitly, to treat most of the world's animals as mechanisms, complex mechanisms to be sure, but unthinking robots nonetheless." Griffin's plea is that animals be studied with empathy, as consciously thinking, sentient beings, not too different from ourselves, a point of view I hold as well.

In a field dominated by competitive birders and professionals there might seem to be little room for amateurs interested in finding out for themselves how birds live. Nevertheless I feel there are a huge number of people who love birds and nature in simpler ways than either the birders or the scientists. This book, based on nearly forty years of watching bird behavior, will, I hope, be a step to approaching nature in a way that these readers will find intellectually and esthetically satisfying as they seek to learn about the other creatures with whom we share this planet.

ONE

FORMATIVE YEARS

JUSTICE OLIVER WENDELL HOLMES said, "I used to tell my students they could do anything they wanted, if only they wanted to hard enough. But what I did not tell them was that they must be born wanting to." I think I was born wanting to be with animals and nature. It was my family's summer place in Tamworth, at the edge of the White Mountains in New Hampshire, that drew out my interest at an early age. I was the youngest of six children, and all of us were devoted to the place. Its history was a bit unusual. One of my father's first jobs as a young architect in Boston was to do over a house for a friend in Tamworth. He went up there in winter to see the house, and my mother, who had been brought up in San Francisco and studied painting in Paris, went along with him. The two went snowshoeing and, coming to an abandoned town road, followed it for a quarter-mile to the remains of an old farm. The house, built in 1790 with huge hand-hewn beams that still stood intact, had doors and windows that were open to the breezes and neighbors' cows. Outside was a wonderful view of the mountains, from Chocorua with its rocky peak to Sandwich Dome. My mother was entranced. She was devoted to painting landscapes and still lifes, she loved gardening, and the beauty and isolation of "The Clearing" appealed to her.

I had two older brothers, Walter and Peter. (Peter later founded Droll Yankees, Inc., a designer and manufacturer of bird feeders.) We were all interested in nature, but our interests

1

manifested themselves in different ways. My brother Walter was seven years older than I. He was tireless in whatever he undertook, including climbing mountains with or without trails. Following him when I was seven to ten years of age has left me with memories of what it is like to be hungry, thirsty, and bone tired. I have, nonetheless, always enjoyed camping and mountain climbing and, due to my early experiences with Walter, have never worried about wandering away from trails wherever I have been, whether in the Rockies or in tropical rain forests.

My early experiences with Peter usually involved ponds. Beginning when I was six or seven Peter and I used to get up at 4:00 A.M., eat cold cereal, then trudge four miles over dirt roads to Bearcamp or some other pond and fish all day in a square-ended, leaky boat which we poled about and had to bail out with a tin can. It was amazing how time passed. I never tired of looking into the water and pulling up an occasional perch or sunfish, while Peter cast for pickerel. At the end of the day we would start the trek back home with our strings of fish. By that time our mother, beginning to be worried about us, would usually send someone to look for us in the family's first car, a 1916 Dodge.

A pond closer by our house in Tamworth became something of an obsession with me and remained so for many years. This was Jackmond or, as we always called it, Cowskull Pond. Three quarters of its shore was floating bog of sphagnum and leatherleaf bushes interspersed with pitcher plants and arethusa. Out from shore were myriads of water lilies.

Cowskull's greatest attraction was the number of painted turtles it contained. I was not allowed to go the pond alone, because of the danger of what the natives called the "stick mud," but when I could get my father to walk there with me on one of his weekends up from Boston, I would creep along the shores catching as many turtles as I could. What I wanted were small ones that I could keep in an aquarium along with water weeds from the pond. Small turtles were difficult to find and always a prize.

The outlet to Cowskull Pond ran under a wooden bridge, through the Bearcamp Meadows to the Bearcamp River. It was in the meadows and on sandy bends of the river that I found wood tortoises, to me one of the most attractive and beautiful of turtles. When I was older my brother Peter made some watercolors of the turtles of Tamworth, and over the years we discussed putting them into a book. My first scientific discovery, if it could be called such, was the finding of a painted turtle moving along a sandy stretch above Cowskull Pond late one afternoon in June, digging a hole, and laying eggs.

I liked catching things, bringing them home, and fixing up places to keep them that were as much like the creatures' natural surroundings as possible. Peter and I discovered that we could catch water snakes with a noose of copper wire at the end of a bamboo pole. A large, thick water snake, we soon found, was a fearsome creature to handle in the way it thrashed about, bit, and smelled. But once tied into a bag it was easy enough to take back to "The Clearing." We built a large exhibition cage for the water snakes, complete with sphagnum moss and plants from the pond where we caught them and to which they were later returned.

Summer people were few in those days, and since I had only one other boy to play with, my summers were spent largely in natural-history rambles, reading, and building a log cabin with Walter. The books I loved especially at this time were *Two Little Savages*, *Lives of the Hunted*, and others by Ernest Thompson Seton.

When I began studying birds at age fourteen, I was fortunate in having Frank M. Chapman's *Handbook of Birds of Eastern North America* and Edward Howe Forbush's *Birds of Massachusetts and other New England States*, the three volumes of which were then just coming out. I remember carrying Chapman's handbook with me into the woods and sitting on a stump to identify a beautiful bird I had seen—yellow on the belly with a black bib, and bright red on throat and crown—a Yellow-bellied Sapsucker! I had made a discovery by myself. If I have carried my boyhood enthusiasm for learning about birds into old age, it is in part because my interest has never been dulled by too many classes, lectures, workshops, meetings, or other experiences that can kill initiative. It is better to learn ten birds on one's own than several hundred following a leader. Learning on one's own is especially important if you want to make discoveries. As Rousseau wrote, "We acquire, without doubt, notions more clear and certain, of things we thus learn ourselves, than of those we are taught by others. Another advantage also resulting from this method is that we do not accustom ourselves to a servile submission to the authority of authors, but by exercising our reason, grow every day more ingenious in the relation of things, in connecting our ideas." Otherwise, he adds, "our invention grows dull and indifferent." Watching birds and other animals for enjoyment should be something that makes us think.

One of Chapman's virtues was that when I looked up a bird in his handbook to identify it, I also learned something of its habits and thus got a start on the bird's life history. In looking up birds in books I was inspired—and still am—by how little was really known about them. From first to last it is discovering that makes studies of any kind exciting. Being the explorer, breaking new ground, is not something that need be limited to a few. It can be the province of anyone, particularly an amateur who takes his education into his own hands. I say "his" by force of habit. I should say "his or her." This is particularly so in the field of bird and mammal behavior, where the majority of the most original and perceptive amateurs in our time have been women.

There are two kinds of discovery. One is finding something really new—a rare occurrence. More often you discover something on your own that later turns out to have been discovered by someone else. I have had this experience, but not nearly as often as I might have expected. It has never discouraged me, because I am out to learn how birds live with my own eyes. If I confirm someone else's work so much the better: it shows that I am on the right track. It is only now and then that I discover something really new.

One of my pleasures in identifying and making lists of birds as a teenager was that I could carry it on during the winter when I was living in Boston. I went birding with two other boys in the

Boston Public Gardens before school as well as to places north and south of Boston where we could find sea- and shorebirds on weekends. One of the boys, a schoolmate, was "Fergie" Locke, later famous for a long run made in the 1934 Harvard–Yale game, and the other, Maurice Broun, became noted later for his work at Hawk Mountain, Pennsylvania, and his book about it, *Hawks Aloft*.

During my first year at Harvard, in 1928, I became fascinated with the university's Museum of Comparative Zoology. How exciting for a mere freshman to meet and talk to such famous ornithologists as Ludlow Griscom. It was a memorable event when, early in my sophomore year, I received a card from Griscom inviting me to breakfast at 5:30 A.M. one Sunday, at his house on Fayerweather Street. I was to go on one of his all-day birding trips up and down the coast of Massachusetts. I felt important riding in a car with well-known bird people, and I was grateful Griscom took me along. I learned many good birding spots, and I saw numbers of new birds. Griscom later had me elected to the Nuttall Ornithological Club. In succeeding years Griscom, aided by Roger Tory Peterson, who was just bringing out his first bird guide, became the great figure who built up the type of birding—pretty much limited to finding rarities, listing species seen, and census taking—that has now become a national pastime. I remember arguments about this new approach to birding back then. The clincher for the Griscom–Peterson type of birding was that it was competitive. Which group at the end of a long, tiring day of car riding would come to a meeting place after dark with the longest list and the fanciest rarities?

By the time I was a junior at Harvard I found my interest in this type of birding wearing thin. The kind of weekend I loved was not using up Sunday driving all day through unattractive cities north and south of Boston, but getting away from Harvard, Cambridge, and surrounding towns by driving up to our cabin in the White Mountains Friday night with one or two college classmates. A lumberman's stove and water from a barn well made "The Clearing" an ideal place to spend weekends in

fall, winter, and spring. We usually arrived after dark. One of
the first things I did, after getting the stove started, was go out
on the lawn and call up my friend, a Barred Owl. The joy of
seeing wild things after a week of lectures—and the exhilaration
of climbing a mountain on a cold November day! I also went on
many weekends to a cabin that my roommate had on Cape Cod.
We walked lonely beaches and sand dunes, and we delighted in
sea- and shorebirds, but we made no great lists. Books that I
liked at the time were books written by observers, people doing
the kind of natural history that I wanted to do; books such as
Henry Beston's *Outermost House* and Charles Wendell Townsend's
Beach Grass. They exemplified an ideal type of natural history:
you lived within walking distance of a beach, marsh, woods, or
mountain and started observing.

Once, during my junior year, I noticed a small snapping
turtle through a hole in the ice in the Charles River and, reaching
down, pulled it up. Arthur Loveridge, curator of herpetology at
the Museum of Comparative Zoology, thought the incident of
sufficient interest to be published in *Copeia*, a journal on reptiles.
My note, "A Snapping Turtle in February," was my first scientific publication and a proud moment.

At Harvard I developed an interest in collecting mammals.
Glover Allen, curator of mammals at the museum, was an unas-
suming, highly intelligent man with a delightful sense of humor. I always looked forward to the occasions when I felt I had
some question that would justify my going through rows of dark
museum cases smelling of moth balls and housing thousands of
specimens from all over the world, to visit Allen in his office.
Collecting revealed a new world to me, a world of small creatures
whose runways ran under stone walls and old logs—red-backed
voles, jumping mice, moles, shrews, and others that I had never
known much about before. I acquired some excellent specimens
of larger mammals—skunks, muskrats, gray squirrels and the
like—when driving back to classes from New Hampshire early
Monday mornings.

One skunk was a particularly fine specimen. After attending

classes for the morning, I went to Arthur Loveridge's office in the museum basement and asked him if he knew where I could skin a skunk. He showed me just the place, a vacant room with a work table and chair. Immersed in my skinning, I kept on for over an hour. What a handsome museum skin my skunk made! I ruptured the scent bag when I started, but as every trapper knows, one's sense of smell soon wears out, and I had paid little attention to the odor. Feeling a bit cramped, I walked to the door for a stretch in the open air. The museum quadrangle was crowded with people. What was going on? The entire staff of the museum was out there. It looked like commencement. Then I felt a tap on my shoulder. It was Arthur Loveridge. "You'd better get out of here quickly. There is an air shaft in that room where you were working, and the skunk smell has gotten into every room in the museum." I headed back for my skunk and made an exit from the other side of the museum as quickly as I could.

My skunk adventure did not end there. Some weeks later I received an official letter with the heading MUSEUM OF COMPARATIVE ZOOLOGY. It was from Dr. Sandground, a parasitologist. I had given him some worms that I had found in the skunk's intestines, and the worms, Dr. Sandground informed me, were of a kind never seen east of the Mississippi. They might be a new species. If so, he asked, could he do me the honor of naming the worm after me?

Halfway through college I switched from being a zoology major to a major in American history and literature. This might seem a surprising change, but when I came to Harvard I had two main interests, which I have retained through life: natural history and the humanities, particularly history and biography. As a boy I was very interested in reading, particularly when I was in Boston and could not get out into the country. My father had a sizable library which included books on American history, and I read a good deal. School meant nothing to me. I could see no relation between it and anything I was interested in. By fourteen I was becoming a bit discouraged. I had five older brothers and sisters who all had more demonstrable talents than I. My mother

was devoted to art and painting, as well as music, and all her
children except me painted, drew, or played some instrument.
Feeling left out, I became somewhat rebellious.

It was against this background that, at age fourteen, I had an
experience that changed my life. It occurred on a rainy day in
August when we were living in Tamworth. I had gone out for a
walk but, seeking shelter from the rain, I entered an abandoned
farmhouse through a back window and amused myself sitting on
the floor of the living room and browsing in some musty-looking
books. The pages in one of them suddenly became very much
alive. The book was one of essays by Emerson. He was a rebel
too. His words in "Self-Reliance" electrified me. "Trust thyself.
Every heart vibrates to that iron string," and "If I am the Devil's
child, I will then live from the Devil." Everyone has something
in him that only he and no one else can do, Emerson insisted. I
might not be able to do what others in my family were doing,
but I could be myself.

The next winter in school I found myself doing well for the
first time. And I found two more heroes, who, like Emerson,
have remained with me. One was Emerson's neighbor, Thoreau,
and the other, Benjamin Franklin, whose *Autobiography* I read in
school. Their ideas of self-education, independence, and the
importance of the mind appealed to me. It was not long before I
added Goethe to my list of heroes. "We find ourselves in others,"
wrote Goethe. This seems to me a very remarkable idea. I was
preconditioned to the thinking of Thoreau, Emerson, and Franklin by my own lonely experiences. It has always seemed a miracle
that men who died long ago should be able to talk to us today
through their books.

At Harvard I found that the men who were curators in the
Museum of Comparative Zoology were men I could talk to. They
were individuals. But when it came to the Department of Zoology, things were different. There was no such subject as the
study of ecology in those days. While I much liked my first
courses, all the higher ones seemed to dissolve into biochemistry.
The instructors and professors, unlike the men in the museum,

seemed to be men of limited interests. In retrospect I think the Zoology Department, as it was then called, was at low ebb at the time I was there. When I switched to history and literature, all was different. My tutor was Perry Miller, and I had many talks with him over the next two years. I had notable teachers in my courses also. One was Bernard DeVoto in advanced composition and another Samuel Eliot Morison in American history. I was glad to learn that Franklin was one of Morison's heroes also; Franklin's wit and sense of humor particularly appealed to him.

Morison lived not far from where we lived on Beacon Hill and, when the two of us were riding on the subway from Cambridge to Boston one day, he invited me to his house for tea. Although regarded as more or less unapproachable at Harvard, he was very friendly to me, and we talked, among other things, about Thoreau. On my leaving Morison's house, he gave me Laura Bridgman's *Stepping Westward* to review for the scholarly *New England Quarterly*, which he edited. This was something of an honor, I felt, for the journal's other reviewers were all professors.

Morison was perhaps the greatest man I met at college. He belonged to a coterie of three men who lived near us in Boston. One was William Morton Wheeler, an authority on ant societies, who was also a noted classicist, and the other, Hans Zinsser, Professor of Bacteriology at the Harvard Medical School and known among literary people for his contributions to the *Atlantic Monthly*. Zinsser was one of the most inspiring men I ever met. His family and mine knew each other, and I had a number of talks with him in his library. He liked to read widely, as I did, and our conversation was always lively. Zinsser got a great kick out of what he did, whether fighting typhus fever in the lab, or being a horseman, or a musician. With his many interests he was, to me, something of an eighteenth-century figure. Zinsser was well acquainted with French and German culture and a believer in the European type of education, which, as he conceived it, was broader than ours. He was the kind of broadly educated, sophisticated man that I did not meet in the Zoology Department—where I later did graduate work, obtaining a Master's Degree. It was Hans Zinsser, and his book *Rats, Lice, and History*, that inspired me after college to go to the Harvard Medical School.

Following medical school I interned at the Lakeside Hospital in Cleveland. It was there that I met my wife, Jane, as a fellow intern. Countries were then toppling right and left before Hitler's triumphant armies. The Battle of Britain was on, and I wanted to go to war. Thanks to Dr. John E. Gordon, Professor of Preventive Medicine at the Harvard Medical School, I received an appointment to the staff of the Harvard–American Red Cross Field Hospital then being erected outside Salisbury, in southern England. I crossed the Atlantic in a blacked-out convoy. My ship had been a floating whale factory. As it pulled out of Halifax, Nova Scotia, five Peregrine Falcons perched in the rigging, the last American birds I was to see for over four years.

Hitler was announcing to the German people that Moscow was about to fall. England stood alone. It was a thrilling place to be. By a fortunate arrangement, Jane joined me in England a few months after I arrived. She served as a physician in the British Emergency Medical Service and was eventually assigned to a hospital in Salisbury, close to the Harvard–Red Cross Hospital where I worked. We both had very good medical experiences. We loved England, met all kinds of people, and birded on bicycles in our spare time. I particularly enjoyed the numbers of winter birds around Salisbury—the skylarks singing, the Lapwing Plovers flying over the water meadows, and the bright-colored finches along the hedgerows. There were two thrilling sounds that we listened to at night. One was the droning of bombers, sometimes German, but mostly British on their way to targets on the continent, and the other, the wailing calls of Stone Curlews, a peculiar type of bird not found in North America.

I eventually joined the army and was attached to a field hospital in Patton's Third Army. Jane sailed for America with our first son, Peter (born in England), at the time I crossed the channel. From the time of the Normandy breakout until we met the Russians in Austria, I could not have wished to be in a better place than Patton's army. Our hospital was never far from the front. We moved fast at times, but there were lulls when nothing much happened. At these times I roamed about the French, Belgian, or German countryside with my field glasses, learning, besides many other things, much about the birds of Europe. When our hospital set up for a week of idleness in the rolling country of Champagne in early September, there happened to be a plague of field voles in the area, and hawks of many kinds— Hen, Montagu, and Marsh Harriers, a kite with a deeply forked tail; and a white bird with a gray mantle, a Short-toed Eagle— were preying on them. In Europe I had a chance to see birds that had been almost eradicated in England.

As we moved on to areas where fighting had been heavier, bird walks were sometimes hazardous. After the Battle of the Bulge I was looking one day for the large Black Woodpecker, a relative of the Pileated, in some woods that sloped up from a river. I found that I could not reach the top of the woods because of a small cliff, but there was a draw where I could climb. Then I paused. What an ideal place for a booby trap! I looked carefully and saw a wire leading across to a hand grenade and two sticks of dynamite.

The German countryside was beautiful in spring. In lulls when we were waiting for our tent hospital to be moved, I found the songs of the spring birds irresistible. Everything on those April days looked so peaceful.

When the war was over, Jane and I settled in Boston, where I began virus research in the laboratory of Dr. John F. Enders. Enders was a very inspiring man. He had gone to Yale, become an instructor in aviation in World War I, then taken up studying Icelandic as a graduate student at Harvard. There he met Hans Zinsser. Zinsser, recognizing Enders' remarkable qualities, suggested that he might find life more exciting studying microbes in the laboratory than Icelandic in the stacks of Widener Library. Enders made the transfer. Zinsser had found a man who was later to win a Nobel Prize for his work on viruses and to become one of the best-known and most-beloved figures at the Harvard Medical School.

I like men I can talk to and Enders was such a man. But he

often had his time taken up with the many people who wanted to
see him. When I had a question, or had found something I
wanted to discuss with him, I usually had to wait. When I did
see him, however, it was as though he had hours to spend. We
talked about the mumps virus I was working on and all the
possibilities that it and other viruses held for the investigator.

Although too much of teachers can dull your appetite for
learning, it is also true that subjects become exciting when you
find a mentor who understands them thoroughly and leads you
on. As a beginner I was not sure what were good problems and
what were not. From the talks I had with Professor Enders, I
gained confidence in what kind of problems I could pursue with
some prospect of success. "Know," advised Carlyle, "what thou
cans't work at." I came to that knowledge from my association
with Enders, and I have remained forever grateful to him. Enders
brought home to me again the significance of Goethe's remark
that "we find ourselves in others."

In 1949 the National Institutes of Health offered me a research position, and, with our two small sons, Jane and I moved
to Maryland's relatively undeveloped suburb of Bethesda. Bethesda seemed incredibly wonderful after Boston. The dogwood
and redbud in bloom, the many birds that came to our yard or
lived not far away, and the mild winters made it seem a naturalist's paradise, one I could enjoy both before and after work, and
on weekends. It was in Bethesda, at almost age forty, that I first
started studying birds and their behavior seriously.

TWO

STARTING OUT

PEOPLE HAVE BECOME students of bird behavior in many ways. In reading A. C. Bent's *Life Histories of North American Birds* I came upon the following remark by Frances Marion Weston: "Our acquaintance with a new bird dates, it seems to me, not from the moment we learn to identify it in the field, but rather from the first time we really have a glimpse of its 'personality.' Thus my first Blue-gray Gnatcatcher was certainly not the one my ornithological mentor pointed out to me, but another that came along months later, flitted to a bush within arm's length of where I stood and, between snatches at insects too small for me to see even at that short distance, spent several minutes looking me over." That's a sentiment I admire. Every bird, as I have found out time and again, can be something special if one will just take the time to really look at it.

My start as a behavior watcher began in no dramatic way. I knew that I wanted to learn more from the wonderful countryside where we lived in Bethesda, and I knew that I must originate some systematic way of doing so. Descartes advised anyone undertaking a new enterprise to begin with what is simplest and easiest, and that is what I did in the early 1950s. Whenever I took a walk or went anywhere, I began observing with the first birds I met. Even if I encountered no more than a few chickadees, I followed them to see how much I could learn before they became lost from view. *Watch everything*, I said to myself: foraging, flocking with other birds, preening, scratching. My system

13

worked from the beginning. I could count on coming home with something learned, something to write in my notes, something to read about, every time I went out. I arranged my notes under families, chickadees under Paridae and Blue Jays under Corvidae, etc. In the dead of winter as well as in summer, and whether my walk was for a half-hour or two hours, my practice was the same. No matter how many experts may have reported on how Blue Jays and chickadees move through the woods, I decided, I must see and discover everything for myself. There is, I quickly found, magic in seeing for oneself. At the same time I started reading up on each bird that I had observed at any length. Observing makes reading mean more, and reading, when it generates ideas, makes you a better observer.

On June 8, 1952, I discovered the nest of a Worm-eating Warbler built more or less under the roots of a small tree that grew on a roadside bank in Seneca, Maryland, a place where I did much of my weekend watching. When I approached the nest a week later, the parents gave sharp *chip*s of alarm, and two young fluttered to the ground. I put them back in the nest and, while I was trying to keep them there, one parent, with wings half open and quivering and crawling like a mouse, came to within six inches of my hand. When I stepped to the dirt road, the parent continued in the same manner, coming to my feet and looking up, but making no effort to lead me from the nest. The other parent carried on in a similar fashion but never came so close. When I walked away, both parents followed for one hundred feet, giving continual *chip*s of alarm. The distance seemed long for so small a bird. On driving by fifteen minutes later, I stopped the car before the warblers' nest. A parent, to my surprise, crawled out from bushes and, with wings quivering, displayed below the car as it had done to me alone.

The Worm-eating Warblers were especially exciting in giving me something to write for publication. Writing a note, even a short one of no great import, can be encouraging to an amateur starting out. What puzzled me then—and still does—was the way the warblers followed me so far, displaying all the way, when I was walking away from their nest. Normally a displaying bird stays in front of an intruder, trying to lead it away.

I had been out for a Saturday morning of natural history along the Potomac River a year later, when I thought to drive to a small reedy pond by the Chesapeake and Ohio Canal. Maybe I would find some Blue-winged Teal or other ducks. The road in was a dumpy affair hemmed in by small trees. When I came to an open place, I stopped. From the pond came the loud *cowp, cowp, cowp, cowp*s of Pied-billed Grebes. I had seen Pied-billeds many times before, but all they had done was swim along, dive, and come up again. Now perhaps, using the car as a blind, I could learn something more.

There were four grebes on the pond in late March, and by watching from 8:00 to 9:00 on Saturday and Sunday mornings for almost a month, I was able to learn something of their courtship. I noted a pair swimming together for a few moments with bills touching, one making loud, rapid *h'n, h'n* notes resembling a nasal laugh. A little later, one grebe flew to another which swam away turning its head from side to side. On April 12 I was surprised to see a single grebe, after remaining in one spot for some time, suddenly stand upright on the surface and beat its wings rapidly while treading water with both feet. Not long after this another grebe, a female, swam to the performer, and the two floated side by side. A few moments later she held her wings out sideways and beat them helplessly on the water. The male then mounted as the two, with much splashing, sank below the surface.

I enjoyed watching by the pond so much that spring that I returned for more observations the following February. For the first month only a single Pied-billed was on the pond. When Coots were diving in open water on March 27, however, a female Ring-necked Duck landed among them. The duck flew suddenly, almost explosively, ten feet over the water as the Pied-billed emerged from the spot where the duck had been. The grebe then swam at the duck, driving it to the other end of the pond. Having rammed the duck from below and chased it over the surface, the grebe gave a series of *ka-ka, cow-cow* calls, the sides of its neck swelling and collapsing as it did so.

I witnessed similar attacks over a number of weekends, the grebe always submerging when about thirty feet from the duck in order to launch an underwater attack. This made for lively watching. Although Coot, Blue-winged Teal, and Wood Ducks came to the pond, it was only the female Ring-necked Duck that the grebe attacked. On April 3, when an immature Pied-billed came to the pond, the grebe attacked it in the same manner as it had the Ring-necked Duck. The Pied-billed was probably a male and defending his territory. He later acquired a mate, enabling me to witness again the courtship that I had seen the year before.

It is not always easy to distinguish the sexes in birds in which the two are *monomorphic*, i.e., alike in plumage. The male Pied-billed at the pond was distinguished by having a lighter back (an individual variation); by being the one to establish territory; by delivering all attacks; by making the only low, prolonged calls; and, on two occasions, by performing the "courtship dance" of standing on the water with rapidly treading feet, a performance that preceded copulation. Once I had identified the male at the time of coition, however, it was easy to follow him because of his lighter back.

I hypothesized that the male Pied-billed Grebe attacked the female Ring-necked Duck, but not other waterfowl, because the female Ring-necked bore a rough resemblance to a Pied-billed Grebe in color pattern, size, and behavior. The Ring-necked is a small duck with a ring on its bill; it is dark brown above and lighter brown below; and, in diving, it lifts its body to an angle of forty-five degrees, thus exposing its white belly. The female Ring-necked Duck thus appeared to have had sufficient behavioral and physical similarities to have aroused aggressivenes in the terrritory-minded grebe.

Our yard in Bethesda was not large, but it had some good trees and at times provided opportunities for behavior watching. Blue Jays had come to a sand pile in the yard in the fall and winter for several years, but it was not until after snowstorms in February

and March that I observed their special attraction to the sand.
Four inches of snow covered the pile one February day and the
jays hopped about as if searching until one of them scooped a hole
by a rock. The others then came to feed. There was no evidence
that they were feeding on anything but sand. Starlings and other
birds coming to our feeders showed no interest in the sand pile,
and the jays did not pick up any objects of appreciable size. On
March 7, I placed some washed sand on a bare log on the sand
pile. A pair of jays came down right away. One picked up one
hundred or more grains or small aggregates. Two other jays then
took turns on the log, each taking fifteen to twenty billfuls,
tipping their heads sideways to do so. In succeeding days the jays
were often punctual in coming at 6:35–6:40 A.M.. It seemed
from these observations that Blue Jays eat sand regularly in
winter, presumably to aid in the digestion of grain, acorns, or
other hard winter fare.

There is fun in learning for yourself what birds live on,
and a yard, especially in winter, can be a place to learn and experiment. Years later, when feeding about seventy-five crows
through the winter on a neighbor's farm in New Hampshire, I
noted that they flew over snow-covered fields every morning to
feed on sand by a roadside. As with the jays, I could find nothing
in books about their need for sand in winter.

In our house in Bethesda on November 13, 1953, I heard a light
thud as a White-breasted Nuthatch struck a picture window and
fell to the ground. I ran out to find it clinging to the base of a
post, panting with its bill open. I was nearly able to catch it
before it flew to the limb of a tree, looking dazed. A second
nuthatch attacked it immediately, delivering some hard blows. I
might have forgotten the incident had I not chanced to see a
relevant note by R. C. Fleming some years later. Fleming, in
contrast to my experience, saw a White-breasted Nuthatch
spend some minutes beside another that had been stunned or
killed by striking a window, in what seemed to be altruistic
behavior.

While the above observations are simple ones, they raise the question of whether birds or animals are apt to attack one of their own kind that is injured, the way lions of a pride may attack one that has been shot. The question is a provocative one, and more observations are needed to settle it. I have been able to find little on the subject except William Brewster's observation, made from a window, of a male Downy Woodpecker attacking an injured female so savagely that he punctured her head ten or twelve times.

When watching by a beaver pond in New Hampshire years later, I happened to be sitting by a thicket where, as I could see by their carrying in insects, a pair of Northern Waterthrushes had a nest. When I moved, one of the pair made five feigned injury or distraction displays on bare ground next to me, crawling with wings arched as if crippled. On its last four runs it was sharply attacked by its mate and driven away. Northern Waterthrushes nest amid low vegetation where the parent would have displayed under usual conditions. I wondered if, when one of the pair crawled about in the open as if crippled it ceased to put out normal signals, and so was attacked by its mate as being an alien intruder.

Striking windows is a common phenomenon, and almost any yard owner is in a good position to make observations on how birds react to injured birds of their own kind.

Some bird lovers become upset by squirrels coming to their feeders. My own reaction is one of tolerance: if you can't lick 'em, join 'em. There are not many mammals that one can watch conveniently, and when we lived in Bethesda I made friends with three gray squirrels, one of them a black individual. I fed them every morning on our back porch before going to work. It was fun taming the squirrels, and I soon had them coming to my lap. Thinking to learn more, I put up a squirrel box on a pole. A female squirrel came to our yard in February and became tame to the extent of following me about and taking peanuts from my hand. She took over my box in early March, and I suspected that she had young.

Jane and I were awakened at midnight on March 28 by the

caterwauling of a Barred Owl coming from the corner of the yard where the squirrel nested. We both thought the caterwauling blood-curdling. I never saw the mother squirrel again, and two and a half days later the motherless young fell out of the box. I picked them up and found them feeble and starving. It is possible that the mother had been seized when emerging from the nest in the night to get rid of excreta. I had seen a mother squirrel moving about in the middle of the night the year before. But why, if the owl had seized the squirrel, had it made such a fearful noise?

The caterwauling of Barred Owls is one of the most thrilling vocalizations you are likely to hear in northern woods. As the noted ornithologist William Brewster wrote of camping in northern Maine in September 1896, "We were suddenly awakened about mid-night by outrageous squalling, snarling, growling coming from somewhere close to the tents and exactly like that of tomcats engaged in nocturnal strife but much louder." The outcry was followed, from the same place, "by the normal hooting of a Barred Owl." On the basis of one episode I could not go far in connecting the death of the squirrel with the owl's caterwauling, but the connection, such as it was, interested me. I kept it in mind until, sixteen years later, I ran into another owl-squirrel encounter which seemed to cast some light.

I was at my desk at the Dartmouth Medical School at 1:00 P.M. on January 13, 1969, when the telephone rang. An excited lady said that she had just been driving by the Bema, a wooded park belonging to the college, when she heard a tremendous racket, like "the screaming of a hundred Blue Jays." At the same time she saw a large owl on the snow by the street. She thought it was hurt and called the school for help. I rushed out, possibly reaching the bird within ten minutes of the time the lady had first seen it. What I found was a Barred Owl. I approached slowly, wondering if I could capture it. But, to my surprise, the owl took wing, appearing in perfect condition as it flew off bearing a large gray squirrel. The squirrel was so heavy that the owl could barely rise six feet above the ground.

I tried to reconstruct what had happened from signs in the

snow. The squirrel had, apparently, been burrowing as if looking for acorns. There were no signs of any struggle. All I could
find was a simple depression where the owl had rested on top of
the squirrel. The snow round about was white and unstained,
without signs of blood, dirt, fur, or feathers. It thus seemed
unlikely that the owl had either struggled with its victim or had
picked up a squirrel that had been hit on the road by a car.

Why should the owl have rested in an open place, making
itself conspicuous by ear-splitting vocalizations, and why should
the squirrel have died without signs of a struggle?

My hypothesis is that a full-grown gray squirrel is too large for
a Barred Owl to subdue by usual means. A Barred Owl lacks the
powerful talons that enable Great Horned Owls to kill animals as
large as skunks. According to Paul L. Errington, a cottontail
rabbit one-third grown is about the limit of prey size for a Barred
Owl. An adult gray squirrel might be twice as large as an
immature rabbit. It is conceivable, therefore, that Barred Owls
at times resort to other means than simple force to kill their prey.
If an owl struck a gray squirrel suddenly and unawares, at the
same time letting out a blast "like a hundred Blue Jays" in the
squirrel's ears, the squirrel might die of audiogenic seizure or
shock. Such shocks are no fantasy. The Russians have apparently
developed ways of making noises so loud that they can knock out
enemy soldiers. If caterwauling sounds blood-curdling to us at a
distance, think of the explosive effect of an owl's caterwauling
almost in a squirrel's ears. I do not propose that caterwauling
evolved for this purpose. Its primary function seems to be territorial. But that does not rule out that it might, in time, have
become adapted to other uses.

Our decade of living in Bethesda was interrupted in 1954 for two
years when we left to stay first in British East Africa, where I
worked at the Virus Research Institute in Entebbe, Uganda, and
the following year in Hamilton, Montana, where I was stationed
at the Rocky Mountain Laboratory. By this time our family had
increased to five children.

The British let us have a house with large garden. Living right on the equator took a little getting used to. There were strange noises at night. Especially strange were ones coming at dawn and dusk from a tree growing outside our bedroom window. What could they be? Slipping out somewhat before dusk, I was surprised to see two large black-and-white birds flying into our big tree with much whooshing of wings. They were Black and White Casqued Hornbills coming to roost. First they perched side by side. Soon after, the male, recognizable by the large, horny casque on his upper mandible, jerked his head and popped a small fruit from his gullet to the tip of his bill. Then he bent over to feed the "cherry" to his mate. In most tries on this and other evenings she did not accept. Courtship progressed better when she sidled up and he nibbled the feathers of her head and neck. She appeared to enjoy the attention, for her head moved slowly back until it rested on her back and her bill pointed upward. Later she, in turn, preened the male.

From the moment I saw these wonderful birds, which came to our garden every night, I knew that they were what I must study. And what a lucky choice. I followed the hornbills for the next ten months before and after work and at other times. It did not take long to find that they were going to nest in a big arching tree limb in the botanical garden in Entebbe. Sitting at the top of a steep bank, I could look at the nest hole at eye level, observing in detail how the male brought his mate dirt from termite mounds, moistened it with saliva, and gave it to her in pellets with which she gradually walled herself into the nest cavity. She was not to emerge until 119 days later. She then knocked the wall away and came out along with a well-grown young one, the male having brought food to her during her long period of confinement, passing it through a slitlike opening in the wall.

A lesson I learned from the hornbills was that I succeed best with opportunistic studies, topics that fit in with the country where I am living and the work I am doing. Hornbills came to our garden daily, so I could watch foraging and other behavior as well as roosting without going out of my way, and the nearby

botanical garden, being largely open, made an ideal place for watching the nest. Recognizing the right place for operations is something that behavior watching has in common with the art of war. Hannibal's successes over the 'Romans were largely due to his eye for terrain. The behavior-watcher who finds a highly favorable place will be able to make more and better observations than the student who is not particular in picking his spot. Although, as an amateur, I find opportunism the best way to study birds and the most enjoyable way of doing so, professionals, with different purposes in mind, generally travel abroad to study some definite project, as exemplified by David Lack's classic on Darwin's Finches in the Galapagos Islands.

I got a feeling for Africa that was very satisfying by studying one bird at length, but I was not sedentary there. Jane, the children, and I took safaris to Kenya, Tanzania, and the Congo in our Ford Ranchwagon. It is all too easy when abroad to hurry, hurry, hurry—the feeling being that one has to look at as much as possible and move on. Sitting in one place and observing carefully, I find, leads to a deeper understanding. I like to have something that I have really come to know, reflect upon, and write up when I get home. The hornbills were the longest study I had made on bird behavior up to that time. In addition to the Entebbe pair, I studied nests in the Mpanga Forest, near Entebbe, on weekends, following as many aspects of their lives as I could to round out my African studies.

The first night we got back to our house in Bethesda after nearly a year in Africa, curiously, the Barred Owls in our backyard, as if welcoming us home, did a tremendous amount of caterwauling. The next morning a neighbor, who took a somewhat dim view of wildlife, spread the word that I had brought home some "buzzards" from Africa that were the cause of all the "hollerin'" in the night.

We had hardly returned to Bethesda in 1955 when I was told I was being transferred for a year to the Rocky Mountain Laboratory—a grand place for wildlife. In Montana I became diverted by mountain climbing and hunting bighorn sheep, mountain goats, elk, and other game with a camera "gun" that my brother Walter designed for me. I did not do as much behavior watching as I would have liked, but I did have one unusually good experience.

There were two mountain ranges in the Bitterroot Valley where we lived: one to the west with jagged peaks, the Bitterroots; and one to the east, the Sapphire Range, with lower, rounded hills. I was driving into the Sapphires one morning when I came to a brook surrounded by meadows and Douglas fir. It looked like a good place for birds, so I got out to look around. A sharp *caack* pierced the air, and I recognized it as coming from a pika. Pikas are short-eared, short-legged relations of rabbits. I found a colony of them living in a rockslide. I supposed that the *caack* was a note of alarm. But was it? I had never sat down to watch pikas. Why not stop for a while to see what they did and what the note might mean? Thus began a series of visits that lasted for five weeks until snow blocked the roads.

In the early morning the pikas were generally busy running to the fringes of the rockslide to cut stalks of grass, twigs, or other vegetation, then racing back to brush piles with the cuttings projecting from their mouths. The piles consisted of items ranging from cones and clumps of moss to sprigs of Douglas fir. There was much individuality in the way the pikas made brush piles. Some hid their piles under rocks, while others placed theirs in the open. The latter practice had its dangers. The pika nearest to where I sat had some sizable piles at the foot of the rockslide. One morning they were gone. It did not take long to discover, by tracks and droppings, that a moose had eaten them. The pikas that hid their piles under rocks had reasons for doing so.

I was pleased to find that the pikas living in the rockslide were molting and recognizable individually by their patterns of brown and gray fur. Six of them lived in the slide. I found from continued watching that each had a territory and, when not harvesting, perched on a lookout where it could watch over its domain.

I obtained a clearer idea of what the pikas' *caack* meant on October 8, 1955, when I watched one pika invade the territory of another. The latter ran toward the invader, who immediately headed back the way it had come. The other pika continued to a rock where its intruding neighbor had perched and called *caack* a number of times. Then it raced back to its brush piles. I believed that the *caack*s advertised ownership, a warning to neighbors to keep out.

That the *caack* was not an alarm call was further suggested when a longtail weasel came by the pikas' rockslide on two successive mornings. It hunted persistently, running in and out among the logs and rocks and occasionally raising its head and neck or even standing on its hind legs to peer about. Although a number of pikas remained in the open, not a single one made a *caack*. The call was clearly not one of alarm.

The pikas marked their territories by leaving their droppings and urinating on their brush piles as well as by stopping occasionally to rub both cheeks against rocks. After my note on pikas appeared in the *Journal of Mammalogy*, a zoologist wrote asking how I had known that pikas had cheek glands. He had been investigating pikas for some years but did not know what the glands were for. I answered that I did not know that pikas had cheek glands, but I inferred they had from their behavior.

The pikas were ideal for watching. They lived on an open rockslide with no bushes to hide their activities. They called attention to themselves by their vocalizations and were marked individually, thanks to their molting. Another advantage to studying them was that, because they are territorial, I could count on their being in the same places weekend after weekend.

It turned out that no one had studied territories in pikas before, and my observations led to a number of studies by others. Even if all the facts had been known before I started, however, I would have watched the pikas anyway. Watching them on the rockslide was an an enjoyable experience, especially as the slide was located in a beautiful place with a brook, a meadow, and Douglas firs.

Readers may wonder why, in a book on watching bird behavior, I occasionally give an account of watching some mammal. I feel that it does not pay to be too narrowly oriented. Some diurnal mammals, as the pikas illustrate, can be watched in the same manner as birds, and if, in a particular locality, you find a good opportunity to study some mammal and nothing particularly favorable with birds, why not be guided by chance? Audubon studied and painted both mammals and birds, and anyone interested in conservation should consider all living things. Watching animals can also lead to observations of birds. In the account of the caterwauling of the Barred Owls, and in the following sketch of the sweeping of nesting White-breasted Nuthatches, it was an interest in a mammal, the gray squirrel, that led to some of the more interesting discoveries I have made in years of studying bird behavior.

On our return to Bethesda from Montana in 1956, and some years after putting up my first squirrel box, I put up another, not on a pole but on the trunk of a large tree, little suspecting that it would provide me with several months of interesting watching. When a female White-breasted Nuthatch started carrying bits of bark and other nest material into the box on April 10, 1961, I was puzzled by her stopping every so often to sweep the roof and the bark of the adjacent tree with her bill. The bouts might go on for five or more minutes at a time. When her mate arrived with food on one occasion she paid no attention but went on sweeping. A few minutes later he arrived with an insect and used it in the manner of a broom to sweep inside, then outside the entrance of the squirrel box, until almost nothing of the insect remained. Both nuthatches acted, at times while they were sweeping, as if possessed. The female swept less during incubation, but the male swept so vigorously at midday on May 2, the day incubation began, that I could hear the *swish, swish* sixty feet away. On May 6 both nuthatches swept continuously from 7:08 to 7:18 P.M., particularly on the roof and corners of the nest box as well as on knoblike growths on the nearby tree trunk, paying little attention to each other and making no vocalizations. At 7:25 the two returned to sweep even more vigorously than before. The female then entered the box for the night, and her mate, after two minutes of frantic sweeping, left to roost elsewhere. The pair continued to sweep during the nestling period, especially as evening came on.

In June 1961, when I joined the Dartmouth Medical School faculty, we packed up to move to Lyme, New Hampshire, and it was some years before I observed the nesting of White-breasted Nuthatches again. In studying five pairs over a number of years, I noted that they swept with insects in their bills, or even crushed, juicy-looking bits of vegetation. There were several occasions when a squirrel in a neighboring tree served to intensify the sweeping. White-breasted Nuthatches nest in natural cavities, often in sugar maples, and preferably in ones with entrances larger than their body size. My hypothesis about their sweeping is that tree squirrels which can be predators are also the chief competitors of White-breasted Nuthatches for nest cavities, and that sweeping, with insects or vegetation containing repellent substances, serves to deter or deflect squirrels from entering. An initial difficulty for this theory was that I found it difficult to determine what the insects actually were that the nuthatches swept with. I noted on two occasions, however, that when a female nuthatch came to her nest carrying a metal-blue beetle three quarters of an inch long, she seemed impelled to sweep intensively both inside and outside her nest cavity. Although I was unable to find any similar beetles in the woods, Jane, the following May, announced that she had found considerable numbers of them in a dry field where the beetles had gathered to mate. They were blister beetles and appeared to be exactly like those I had seen the nuthatches using the year before. I offered several to a pair of hand-raised nuthatches breeding in my aviary. The female, seizing one, began sweeping immediately inside and outside her nest cavity in the same manner I had noted in the field the year before. She was incubating eggs and had no nestlings to feed. I had given her miscellaneous beetles in the past without being able to precipitate sweeping. Indeed, over two years of trying to breed nuthatches in captivity, I had not been able to induce the sweeping I had observed in the wild.

Blister beetles, as I found on handling them, exude a copious, oily, blister-inducing fluid from their leg joints. My captive nuthatches were, unfortunately, unable to hatch their eggs, and I was unable to make further observations. The sweeping of nuthatches needs further investigation, and blister beetles might facilitate further observations and experiments, since they are available in numbers and are easily recognized. The blistering agent, a well-known and powerful drug known as "cantharidin," is present in the beetles' blood and in more concentrated form in the reproductive organs. It might, therefore, be liberated in considerable amounts from a crushed beetle used in sweeping. To me this entire pattern of behavior is very exciting. It indicates again what a vast amount remains to be discovered about our commonest birds.

As in other aspects of behavior-watching, an individualized pursuit, devotees will vary in methods, tactics, and the amount of equipment they like to use. There is no one way of observation. As Nietzsche said of philosophy, "This is my way. What is yours? As for the way, there is no such thing." I lean toward working with a minimum of equipment, for example, but I realize that others, more gadget-minded than I, will prefer to work with more. All one needs for watching is a pair of binoculars and a pen and paper for note-taking. To these I would add a folding chair that is easy to carry. One of the many advantages of a chair, whether one is young or old, is that it makes one sit still. The trouble with most men, said Pascal, is that they cannot sit still in a room alone. I would say that the trouble with many would-be behavior watchers is related: they can't sit still out of doors. Being comfortable in a chair has a settling effect. It helps make one content to stay in one place and watch, especially during periods, which always occur, when nothing much happens.

I use two pairs of binoculars: 8 x 40s for birds at close range and a large pair, 11 x 80, for viewing crows, ravens, nesting Red-shouldered Hawks, and other large birds at a distance. A large pair of binoculars is much easier to look through than a telescope, lets in more light, and has a larger field of view.

Taking notes is the *sine qua non* of being a good observer. Notes are usually best taken at the time of making observations or shortly thereafter, but here again watchers will vary. I like to scratch down notes rapidly in the field when a good deal is going on, knowing how frustrating it can be to find out later that I cannot recall something that I was sure I could remember. By making only rough notes in the field, I am not too distracted from what the birds or animals I am watching may be doing. Once home, I rewrite my notes, indexing them with, for example, a 1 for territory, a 2 for vocalizations, and so forth. Since I am interested in learning everything about the birds I am studying, I take notes on how they preen, move over the ground (walk, hop, or run), and fly. I also note details of their foraging, courtship, nesting, vocalizations, and other behaviors.

A valuable part of going over field notes while they are fresh is that it prompts you to reflect upon what the birds were doing and to ask questions. Going over notes can generate ideas. Sometimes I realize that a behavior that did not seem like much at the time could be important. I had better look more carefully the next time. This process has, on a number of occasions, led me to something interesting that I might have missed otherwise. Note-taking makes a good observer.

Photographic equipment has reached a high state of perfection, and expert wildlife photographers are legion. Nevertheless, few people have been able to be good behavior watchers and take photographs at the same time. Behavior-watching, when one is in the field, is a full-time job. If one is trying to take a good picture, he or she will not be concentrating on what a bird is doing. Important things in the life of a bird can happen in seconds. Photography is a full-time occupation, and so is behavior-watching. I carry a small, automatic-focusing camera in my pocket but usually use it only after I have finished making observations for a morning or afternoon. I have used a very convenient Sony Walkman tape recorder at times but have been dismayed by how much behavior I have missed when trying to use it. Watchers more technically oriented than I will disagree with me, I am sure, but I feel that the combination of mind and eye plus other sense organs is a greater piece of apparatus for observing, thinking, and discovering than any computerized gadget. The human brain evolved, not in Silicon Valley, but in the millions of years during which our ancestors lived as hunters to whom watching animals and learning their ways was essential to survival. Rousseau claimed that "the more ingenious and accurate our instruments, the more unsusceptible and inexpert become our organs: by assembling a heap of machinery about us, we find afterwards none in ourselves."

I have never banded birds and have never felt the need of doing so, partly because I have avoided detailed studies on such birds as Blue Jays and Red-cockaded Woodpeckers, in which bands might be essential. It is obvious that there are many important studies that could not have been carried out had birds not been banded or otherwise marked individually. On the other hand, as I remark elsewhere in this book, many species whose members appear to look alike on first view can be found to have individual marks if carefully observed; hence banding will be unnecessary. I feel that banding birds is far from providing an answer to all questions. When observing woodpeckers that someone else had banded, I found that it took too much time to get a view of the band when I needed to see it most, that is, when something exciting was happening and there was simply no time to fool around looking for a leg band hidden by the bird's body. Another thing about banding that distresses me is that there have been far too few studies on the effects of banding on birds. Climbing to nests or trapping in mist nets, letting a bird struggle there for hours, then capturing and banding it, subject birds to stress that could distort their behavior. I feel surer of what I am doing if the birds I am observing have been as little disturbed as possible.

THREE

WOODPECKERS NORTH AND SOUTH

I WAS WALKING near the Chesapeake and Ohio Canal in Maryland in September 1956. Would I, I wondered, ever be able to find birds as engrossing as the hornbills I had watched in Africa? There I had had much to watch every month. Back home, how could I find enough birds to keep me busy in winter? I feared that I was in for a letdown. With such thoughts I paused to watch some Red-headed Woodpeckers. They were coming to a large pin oak to harvest acorns. Blue Jays were trying to rob them. What a colorful spectacle! Then an idea came to me. Why go farther? Why not study these birds? Keep with them, I said to myself, and something will turn up.

Nothing much happened on the next three to four weekends. Each woodpecker kept flying to clusters of acorns, picking one, then flying to some stub to poke it into a crevice. If I did not see much, however, I enjoyed being out in a beautiful place, watching the fall colors, and learning small things. But when leaves began to fall in October and I could see into the woods, things suddenly became more interesting. I now discovered that there were twelve Red-headed Woodpeckers living in a clump of woods four acres in extent, surrounded by fields. The fields enabled me to see that the woodpeckers almost never flew out of their wood, so busy were they inside. Another advantage of the wood, Creek Wood, as I called it, was that its sides sloped down to a creek, enabling me to look into the wood at midtree levels. I was thus able to work out that each Red-headed had a small territory in which it cached hundreds upon hundreds of acorns from pin oaks bearing a bumper crop. Each woodpecker stored and restored its harvests, putting acorns in deep cavities and crevices.

The woodpeckers made rattling *kwirr*s when other birds with a taste for acorns came through the wood. Among intruders driven out were chickadees, Tufted Titmice, and Blue Jays, as well as Downy, Hairy, and Red-bellied Woodpeckers. From noting where conflicts took place and what the limits of the usual flights of each woodpecker were, I was gradually able to make a map of the wood showing the boundaries of the territories it contained.

It is important in any study to recognize birds individually. This was not possible with the Red-headeds at first, for they are monomorphic. But with months of watching I came to recognize behavioral differences which revealed that each woodpecker spent almost its entire time within its own territory.

On a dark, damp Saturday in early November, as I checked my woodpeckers in Creek Wood, I noticed something I had not seen before. One woodpecker, then another flew to the ground, pulled a good-sized sliver from a rotting log, the sliver so wet that it drooped from the bill, then flew to some dead stub and pushed the sliver into a hole or crevice. I could make no immediate sense of what the woodpeckers were doing. Three weeks later I saw the woodpeckers collecting wet slivers again. I now realized that, as earlier in the month, they were doing so on the morning after a heavy rain. Could the Red-headeds be using the wet wood to seal in their stores of acorns? I brought along a ladder and a saw on my next visit and, with the help of my son Mike, began examining the storage trees. We soon found that the wet slivers, which were like *papier mâché* to start with, had been pounded into holes leading to pockets containing dozens of acorns. When bits of bark were incorporated with the slivers, it was difficult to locate where the stores were.

The Red-headeds had several ways of supplementing their diet of acorns in winter months. One was to perch on the very tops of the oaks on warmer winter days to catch passing insects on the wing, and another was to dig special pits in tree bark as a way of getting sap. This was a surprise, for I had supposed hitherto that only sapsuckers, among woodpeckers, took sap from trees by their own exertions.

The Red-headeds remained on their territories until early May 1957. They were, it seemed, migratory opportunists. Having spent the fall, winter, and much of the spring where they had found a bumper crop of acorns, they left as the breeding urge came on to breed elsewhere.

My eight-month study from September 1956 to May 1957 was lucky in many ways. In addition to learning much about Red-headed Woodpecker behavior I had made the new and incidental discovery that Red-bellied, Downy, and Hairy Woodpeckers began their breeding seasons in winter. This was a major discovery. It meant that for years to come I could go on discovering things about birds in winter months, such as the onset of drumming and its meaning, territorial conflicts, and courtship. With these possibilities in view, I went on to the idea of making a comparative study of the woodpeckers of eastern North America.

When following the Red-headeds in Creek Wood, I heard loud *kwirr, kwirr*s coming from a neighboring swamp on some winter mornings and not others. Why should Red-bellied Woodpeckers be making so much commotion in the dead of winter? Wanting to know more, I crossed the road and entered the swamp early on the morning of February 3, 1957. The calls of one male led me to a silver maple with a hole sixty feet up. Just as I arrived the male flew into the hole to rest with his head out. *Kwirr, kwirr, kwirr*, he called, then dropped from sight. To my surprise—for I knew little of Red-bellied Woodpeckers at the time—he began giving slow, clear taps from within the tree as his mate came flying through the woods. She alighted by the hole, and the two tapped together, she on the outside and he out of sight on the inside. I called this ceremony, which I was to see

many times later on, "mutual tapping." The male put his head
out again as soon as his mate left. He now called *kwirr* eight
times, pointing his bill toward the ground each time to display
the flaming red feathers of his crown. He soon dropped from
sight to tap as his mate again flew to his roost hole to join in
another round.

I had never dreamed that woodpeckers could have such a
colorful ritual. Fascinated, I returned to the silver maple early on
the mornings of February 10 and 13. It became clear that the
female was accepting, at least as a starter, the male's roost hole as
a possible nest hole. Otherwise she would not have continued
flying to him and tapping. But by February 16 she was beginning to have doubts. My first intimation of this was her *quer*s
coming from a different hole which she had moved to by the
Chesapeake and Ohio Canal. Her mate tried with his usual
*kwirr*s to entice her to return to the silver maple, but she would
not come. By February 24, seemingly in an effort to please her,
he was excavating a new hole by the canal in the direction she had
moved a week before.

A second round of courtship and tapping had begun by the
time I returned the next morning. The male Red-bellied put his
head out of his new excavation at 6:40 A.M. to give a few low
*kwirr*s. His mate answered immediately with her flatter *quer*s,
flying to him as he dropped out of sight within the tree. She
tapped, but I did not hear him. I think he didn't tap because his
new excavation was not deep enough, as yet, to allow him to
maneuver inside. I observed with other pairs of these woodpeckers that, at the very start of an excavation, before the male could
enter, both members of a pair might tap side by side below it.
However done, the tapping registers agreement on a nesting
site. Like most woodpeckers, Red-bellieds prefer to excavate a
fresh hole each year. The male may try early on, as did my first
male, to get the female to accept his winter roost hole. The
female woodpeckers are nearly always the most particular of the
two, however, and will not accept just any hole of a male's
choosing.

Discovery of tapping and its meaning was one of the big excitements of my first winter of studying woodpeckers. The blows in tapping, as distinct from drumming, are delivered at a regular, countable rate of about 2.3 taps per second with 4–20 taps in a burst. I was to find later that all species of woodpeckers, at least all those I have studied, tap in relation to choosing nest sites. With most species, however, only one of a pair taps at a time. Red-bellieds are the most dramatic in tapping together, but another species does so too.

Red-headed Woodpeckers are related to Red-bellieds, and I wondered, in my first winter with the woodpeckers, whether they might also tap simultaneously. The Red-headeds of Creek Wood left in May 1957 to breed elsewhere, however, and I was unable to find out. Still curious, I made a special trip to Florida in May two years later. Staying at the Archbold Biological Station, I went out at dawn to some burnt pine lands with many weathered stubs still standing. There I heard the loud *quee-rk*s of a breeding male Red-headed Woodpecker. The Red-headed was looking out from his roost hole. When, after a number of desperate sounding *queeark*s his mate finally flew to him, he dropped out of sight and, in a few seconds, the two were tapping together—in the same manner as the Red-bellieds had tapped mutually in their swamp by Creek Wood. My hunch had proved correct.

Learning how birds communicate with each other in the breeding season when so much is going on is one of the more fascinating aspects of studying their behavior. Woodpeckers, which communicate by drumming and tapping as well as by varied vocalizations, are a particularly rewarding group in which to observe communication. The key to what a woodpecker or other bird is communicating lies in attendant circumstances. Interpreting these is not always easy, but it has often been surprising to me, if I have followed birds through a number of breeding seasons, how questions eventually have found answers.

While we lived in Maryland I was unable to go to the woods where I studied woodpeckers on weekdays, so I decided in the fall of 1958 to see if I could induce Downy Woodpeckers to come to our yard. Not all woodpeckers excavate holes for winter roosting. Downies and Hairies are among those that do, however, and both are choosy about the kind of stubs they excavate. They like stubs of a certain diameter, and they like ones that are decayed but not too much so. With these requirements in mind, I collected a number of fallen logs and wired them to fence posts in our backyard.

My experiment was more successful than I anticipated. Four Downies came to inspect the stubs within a few days. After sounding them out by percussing all around and up and down, they eventually made excavations. There was no difference between the excavations of the Downies in the yard and those I had observed in the wild. In both the digging was done between September and January with a peak in November. The Downies worked especially in the middle of the day. Each, whether male or female, might have a long spell of pecking inside a stub then toss out as many as forty billfuls of sawdust. Every now and then a Downy swung out to percuss around the outside of its cavity. I think this was to ensure that the walls were all of equal thickness.

Times taken to excavate a cavity varied. A female Downy who began excavating on November 1 spent her first night in the hole on the sixth. The consistency of the wood, as well as the urgency of getting a hole ready, made for variations. If there was no urgency a Downy worked only in the middle of the day, but if a bird had lost one cavity and needed another, it might work morning and afternoon. Having a good hole, one with an entrance and cavity that fit a woodpecker's body size, is important to these little birds. A woodpecker that has no roost will have a harder time conserving heat on a cold night, and the better a cavity fits its occupant, the more heat conserved.

A roost hole also protects to some extent against owls and other predators. I did not expect to see any owls in the yard. But in one period of four days our woodpecker population melted away. It was only on the third day that I saw a Screech Owl looking from a box that I had put up for squirrels. When the owl left, the woodpeckers returned. Woodpeckers generally have more than one roost hole. If something goes wrong at one, they can fly to another as darkness comes on.

At this time I was trying to learn all I could about Downy Woodpeckers: how they foraged and defended themselves, what displays they used, their vocalizations, and anything else I could find. I was surprised by how much I learned about Downies from putting up the stubs. I saw not only how they excavated, but also how they defended their holes against other Downies and a variety of hole-nesters ranging from chickadees to Hairy and Red-bellied Woodpeckers. A reason that as many as four Downies came to our small yard is that stubs suitable for excavating are always in short supply. This is true in the woods and even more so in a suburb. Wiring up the semidecayed stubs was a simple experiment. I could watch from the house. I found that Downies, like Hairies, are all individually marked by the patterns of black, white, and, in the case of males, red on the backs of their heads. There was no need for color bands.

When I started studying Downies in New Hampshire in 1967, I walked many miles in the fall and winter woods. Hardly a Downy could I find. It was only by ranging far and wide that I found them concentrating on paper birches of a special kind. New Hampshire has many birches with straight trunks and white bark. These held little attraction for my Downies. What they sought were defective birches, ones crooked or leaning, with broken branches in their crowns and areas of bark blackened with cankers. I was almost sure to find Downies once I found trees of this kind. The trees were nearly always on exposed ridges or slopes damaged by logging.

I couldn't tell what the Downies were feeding on. Here I was fortunate to run across a paper published in 1898. The defective birches, I learned, were trees infested with a coccid, *Xylococcus betulae*. The female coccid is a comparatively large, orange-red, soft-bodied creature that lies in a cavity just under the outer bark. In summer she extrudes a waxy tube and excretes a saccharine honeydew similar to that produced by aphids. In winter she is dormant. The signs of birches infested with these insects are the small trap doors that Downies make in the bark in digging them out. You can find dozens of these markers on a defective birch, for a single tree can harbor hundreds of coccids in places ranging from lenticels to branch stubs. *Xylococcus* infects yellow birches, beeches, and other trees, but it is paper birches that attract Downies the most.

I made repeated visits to a number of stands of coccid-infested birches, but not always successfully. Snow made some inaccessible, and heavy frost coated others, forcing the Downies to feed elsewhere for weeks at a time. I was fortunate in having one area near our home in Lyme, New Hampshire, a boulder slope close to what I called Ben's Swamp, that was both lower and more accessible.

By January 1969 I was following the activities of the Downies on the boulder slope for up to forty minutes at a time, noting their relations to each other and to the parts of trees on which they fed. A circumstance favoring watching was that the Downies did little else except feed on paper birches. After leaving one, they usually flew to another. Of the Downies watched, two were unique in being members of a pair that was to nest by Ben's Swamp in the following spring.

In observing the parts of birches fed upon, I made the exciting discovery, in repeated observations, that the male fed on upper trunks, limbs, and smaller branches, while his mate fed on middle and lower trunks. A typical pattern was for the male to progress up a trunk into the crown, move out along a branch, often clinging upside down until he neared the end, then drop to another branch. He was apt to choose the largest and tallest birches or, if he worked on the trunk, those most blackened by defects.

His mate, in contrast, fed mostly on the middle third of trunks. Here she had to flutter and sometimes fall where smoother bark made clinging difficult. Her mate rarely had to flutter in this way. The places that he fed had rough spots as well as smaller branches that made clinging easier.

One of the most satisfying pleasures anyone can know in

natural history or science is to have his findings confirmed by others. While I was making my observations in New Hampshire, Jerome Jackson was finding that male and female Downies forage in different parts of trees in Kansas. Papers by others followed, showing that sexual differences in foraging are widespread among woodpeckers in both Europe and America. David Ligon, a professional ornithologist, describes sexual differences among Red-cockaded Woodpeckers feeding on pines in Florida that are surprisingly similar to those that I noted for Downies feeding on birches in New Hampshire. Some ornithologists speculate that this "partitioning" of trees, as it is called, spaces woodpeckers out, a kind of insurance against too many foraging in one area.

Hairy Woodpeckers begin drumming in New Hampshire in early January, an indication that their early breeding season—involving territorial conflicts, courtship, and the like—has begun. The place where I watched conflicts was a lonely dirt road where the boundary between the territories of two pairs of Hairies lay. Hairies, like many other birds, rarely come to blows in fighting. The males that I watched, instead of blows, faced each other in bizarre displays in which the performer, with bill pointed upward and white breast displayed, jerked his head and body and half-started his wings as he swung his bill back and forth like a conductor's baton.

I knew where the Hairies roosted and found two males so eager for encounters, on some days, that they flew from their roost holes to their common border without waiting to feed. But they were not alone. Their mates also flew to the boundary, perching farther back and not participating except as spectators. Rather than approaching them as ordeals, the males seemed to enjoy their encounters. The displays were a way of working off steam. I thought of a tennis match, in which both contestants are satisfied to have the boundary, the net, stay where it is. Both play on, spurred by having their mates on the sidelines. If a conflict between the male Hairies by the lonely road continued for an hour, both showed signs of restlessness by pecking here and there. While this might be called "displacement pecking," it also seemed a sign that the birds were actually hungry. They had, after all, had no chance to feed since emerging from their roost holes at dawn.

A feature of the conflicts was that their effects were not limited to the males. The females became aroused by watching, as shown by one or the other taking a copulation pose when their mates flew to them in lulls of fighting. The displays or dances, therefore, were something more than territorial. They were a way of synchronizing the development of sexual drives before actual nesting began.

Following a pair or two of Hairy Woodpeckers the year around gives the watcher, in time, a feeling of being personally acquainted with the birds. Hairies are, next to Pileateds, my favorite woodpeckers. I am always attracted to species like these, which have lifetime pair bonds and show individuality. No two Hairies, no two pairs of Hairies, are exactly alike in behavior. What I saw of courtship and conflict on the New Hampshire dirt road was not something that can be readily duplicated with other pairs.

Many people assume that once birds mate, the romance is over and there is no further need of courtship behavior that year. But those who study bird behavior find that courtship in some species covers a range of activities, strengthening a pair bond in and out of the breeding season. The Pileated Woodpecker is an example. They keep their pair bonds strong with small ceremonies the year around. That's one reason Jane and I were interested in studying Pileateds in places as widely scattered as New Hampshire, Maryland, South Carolina, Florida, and especially on Sapelo, a sea island off Georgia.

It was on Sapelo in February 1974 that I watched the winter activities of a pair that roosted in a grove of loblolly pines. Setting out at dawn, I knew just the spot where, even in dim light, I could get a good view of the male's roost hole. Minutes passed; the hole remained dark and silent. Soon the male looked out and gave a high call, a series of six to eight high-pitched *cuk*s followed by one of lower pitch. Then out he came. Once in a good position at the side of his cavity, he gave a rolling drum. Both the drum and the high call were messages to his mate. She had spent the night some distance away and now gave an answering call.

Day after day I heard the two Pileateds getting in touch with each other soon after sunrise, before they set out foraging on trees, logs, and stumps about the island. The two were seldom more than forty yards apart as they worked on adjacent or nearly adjacent trees. Every so often, one flew to the other. Sometimes the two came close, nearly touching bills, then went their separate ways. Sometimes the female, giving her intimate *woick, woick* vocalization, approached her mate. He would then give way, letting her feed where he had been. Such behavior is unusual among woodpeckers, since males generally supplant females. Male Pileateds do so at times, but signs of dominance are generally few in this species. Male and female Pileateds come close to being equals.

Why should Pileateds move about woods together and feed as a pair? A number of factors may be involved, but it's my hunch that protection against predators is the main reason. When a Pileated is knocking away pieces of bark or excavating wood, it may not be able to look about effectively. Two pairs of eyes and ears are always better than one, especially in these circumstances. Thus, there may be selection in favor of a pair staying together. One Pileated, on seeing a hawk, could alert the other by giving *cuk*s of alarm.

The sun was low over the salt marsh on Sapelo when first the male Pileated, then the female, left on a long flight toward the pine grove where they had started the day. By the time I arrived a Bluebird, dwarfed by the size of the entrance, was inside the male Pileated's roost hole looking out. The female Pileated swooped at the Bluebird, then hitched to the side of the cavity and gave a resounding drum burst. Her mate came right away to alight above. Both birds tapped. The tapping of Pileateds, as for Red-bellieds and other woodpeckers, means attachment to a nest site and attachment of the members of a pair to each other. The hole in the pine had possibly once been a nest, but it was too dilapidated to use again. Possibly it had been the nest of the pair in a previous year. In any case the tapping appeared to be a touch of courtship before the Pileateds separated. The female left and was soon making *cuks* far to the east. The male hitched to his hole, bowed his head in and out several times, then swung in. He gave *cuks* for twelve seconds in response to the *cuks* of his mate in the distance. Then, after looking out briefly, he withdrew and gave a burst of drumming inside his hole. Thus, with a flourish, the pair kept in touch at the last of the day, as they had gotten in touch at sunrise.

Pairs of Pileateds may become involved in territorial conflicts at the end of winter. A juncture of swamp and pines was a boundary where I had earlier watched conflicts between two pairs in Florida. All five conflicts took place in the late afternoon. The Pileateds, making shrill *g-waicks* as they approached their meeting place, were spectacular as they flew from tree to tree or circled trunks, with crests raised and wings out showing their white undersides. Such fighting stimulates a pitch of excitement that does much, seemingly, to strengthen bonds between the members of the pairs involved.

The most severe conflicts are generally over nest sites. A pair of Pileateds were excavating a nest in a dead pine on Sapelo one March, when an intruding male arrived. The female was resting inside the hole. She flew out to attack, and there was much flapping of wings as the two circled the trunk, trying to strike at each other. When the intruder left, the female, seemingly from an overflow of excitement, flew at her mate. The intruder returned a few days later. This time he fought with the male on the trunk of the nest pine, then ascended to the nest hole. The female was again inside. She met the intruder at the entrance, and there was a jabbing of bills. The intruder backed down to attack the male again, then returned to the entrance. Jabbing was now

intense. Feathers flew. Undeterred, the intruder forced his way in on top of the female. After many cackles and scuffles, the female emerged. The intruder had won. But after a time he left. On the following morning, the original pair seemed to have recovered, and I observed the two copulating not far from the nest tree.

Why would an intruder have attacked this pair at their nest hole? Resident birds usually have a psychological advantage over intruders that enables them to win such engagements. The intruder on Sapelo, however, after attacking both members of the resident pair, evicted the female and occupied the nest. A possibility is that, since he had lost his mate at the height of the breeding season, his thwarted energies took to aggression. Partial support for this idea came from the remains of a Pileated that I found earlier near the base of the nest tree. Possibly the intruder had been the one to start making the hole in the first place but had given it up when he lost his mate.

I'd observed this sort of behavior before with the Black-and-White Casqued Hornbills in Africa. There an unmated female came week after week to attack a breeding female walled in her nest. My belief is that Pileated Woodpeckers, like Casqued Hornbills, have lifelong pair bonds. An individual that has lost its mate at the start of a breeding season is, therefore, much affected. He or she may find an outlet by attacking mated pairs that have what the intruder so desperately needs—a nest and a mate.

The courtship of Pileateds, as with most woodpeckers, reaches a peak with excavation of a nest hole. If the male is excavating, his mate may approach, giving low, grunting *hn, hn*s similar to notes of well-developed young. He, seeing her coming, raises his flaming crest, taps at the side of the hole, and flies away as she takes over. Copulations take place as a nest nears completion, usually on a horizontal limb not far away. Sometimes the female gives *woick, woick*s as the two approach, or she limits herself to low *hn, hn*s. On the whole, copulations call forth little in the way of display.

When one of a pair of Pileateds is especially excited about meeting its mate, it bends its head and bill far back, waving them back and forth in an arc of forty-five degrees as it jerks its whole body about in what I call a "bill-waving dance." Pileateds become silent when incubating eggs and brooding but renew courtship as nestlings approach fledging. The female then takes the lead in giving exuberant *woick, woick*s on meeting her mate by or away from the nest.

When I think of the many hours Jane and I have spent watching the courtship of Pileated Woodpeckers in beautiful places such as Sapelo Island, I think how wonderful it is to watch one kind of bird long enough to get to know it well. Such familiarity with a wild creature gives one a feeling of having a bond with nature.

In the same vein, referring to the great movement to preserve natural environments, D. R. Griffin, in his 1984 book, *Animal Thinking*, points out that, "A rarely articulated element in this concern is a feeling that many of the animals we wish to preserve may be sentient creatures whose feelings are worthy of consideration. Among reasons for wishing to preserve nature is our perception of kinship with other animals and our curiosity about their feelings and thoughts."

If one wants to understand animals as consciously feeling, thinking creatures, as Griffin recommends, what aspect of their life is more illuminating than courtship? It is during courtship that birds are most expressive, giving us a good look into how they really live. As subjects for such studies, few birds are more rewarding, beautiful, or conspicuous than Pileated Woodpeckers.

A major consideration in trying to find a bird or group of birds to study is how the project will work out practically for you. What is easiest and nearest is often the best. Margaret Morse Nice became so entranced with the breeding behavior of a pair of nesting Song Sparrows in Ohio that she was led into making a fourteen-year study which became a landmark in the study of bird behavior. All of her studies were made in an extensive weed patch next to her house. Since she was a mother of four and a housewife, convenience meant a good deal. The British ornithologist David Lack also turned to a bird that could not have been more conveniently located. When starting out as a school teacher, he banded robins around the school building to encourage eleven- and twelve-year-olds in science. But he "soon found that each colour-ringed robin held a territory," and this led very gradually into a four-year study. Lack's book, *The Life of the Robin*, made his reputation not only for its scientific worth, but also for the engaging way in which it was written.

D. Summers–Smith, an English businessman, speaking of his amateur study of the House Sparrow, wrote "there were advantages in choosing the House Sparrow, particularly when I was able to devote only a limited time to birds; it is readily accessible and no time had to be wasted in travelling to the 'study area,' observations could be made before breakfast and in the evenings with the minimum of extra effort and my wife could provide continuity in observations when I was away from home. . . . What is more I have been able to make observations on sparrows on all sorts of holidays at home and abroad and even in such unlikely bird-watching localities as railway stations, the inside of factory buildings and from a dentist's chair!" The robin, the Song Sparrow, the House Sparrow, are among the commonest of birds. A bird does not have to be rare to make a good subject for prolonged watching.

Another consideration in selecting a bird to study is whether it is present the year around or only in spring and summer. Specializing on woodpeckers and nuthatches, and later on crows, meant that I could study them in all months and not, as with migrants, only in spring and summer. I have often thought the American Robin would be a good bird for special study. Few birds are more commonly at hand and therefore more studiable. But, living in New Hampshire, I would only be able to study the robin from March until late summer. A study of warblers would be even more limited. A further limitation, which I find I am not alone in having, is that I have developed high-tone deafness with age. While I can no longer hear the songs of birds that I once knew well, I can hear the vocalizations of crows and ravens, my speciality. The woodpeckers and nuthatches, when I studied them, were also birds that I could hear.

David Lack, Margaret Morse Nice, and Summers–Smith all studied single species. What especially attracted me to woodpeckers was that they consisted of a variety of species within a relatively small group. If I could not find any very suitable nests of Downy Woodpeckers in any one spring, I could turn to Hairies, or sapsuckers, or flickers, depending on which species offered the best opportunities. With six to seven woodpecker species to choose from, I could keep myself busy twelve months a year with one project or another. Although this meant some jumping around on a short-term basis, in the long term of twenty-four years, I was able to make relatively complete observations on all of the available woodpeckers.

Another advantage to studying a group—a considerable one—is the opportunity of making comparisons. What I learned about one species gave me ideas on what I might be looking for in others.

A bird watcher, however, does not have to make a prolonged study of any bird or group of birds to begin with. As most of the cases in this book illustrate, making short studies of varied species, when you have a special opportunity to do so, can keep you profitably occupied. Small studies have a number of advantages. They are one of the better ways to begin as a behavior watcher, for it may be difficult to decide on a prolonged project until you have some background of experience.

Small studies can also have advantages for anyone who has been watching for years. Extended projects tend to run out in time. After working on woodpeckers for twenty years I found I was begining to get stereotyped in the way I looked at them. I had become something of an expert, or was regarded as such, but I was not having as many new thoughts or or seeing as many new things as when I started. When a project runs into that stage, it is time to go on to something else. Don't allow yourself to become fossilized. A way to prevent this is to keep a few small studies going all the time, on a back burner, as a way of maintaining broader interests. One of the saddest things in science is to see scientists who have run out of things to do. The way to keep alive, whether as a scientist or an amateur, is to maintain interests in many things.

FOUR

READING FOR IDEAS AND INSPIRATION

IT IS SAID that reading rots the mind, and the philosopher Alfred North Whitehead remarked that "the merely well-informed man is the most useless bore on earth." I am apt to think of these remarks when I see a graduate student glued to a pile of scientific journals for hours at a time. Reading is a poor way to start yourself on a scientific project, if you want to be original and a discoverer. Go out into the field and build up some unprejudiced observations of your own—*then* reading becomes a different matter. You have a live interest in something. This alternation of looking things up in books with observations in the field is one of the most fruitful ways of stimulating your thinking. And a background of reading, built up over years, is a great help in sustaining interest.

Robert Frost urged students to start a library. He felt so strongly about this that he offered an A to any student buying a hundred and a B to any buying fifty dollars' worth of books. Nothing was a sadder sight to Frost than to enter a bookless home. I have a comparatively large library, because for me a book in the hand, one I can underline and take up at any time, is worth a dozen in a college or public library. To get at information when you want it, that's the thing. I have, say, been out in the field and seen something odd with my woodpeckers. Has anyone seen the phenomenon before? I take A. C. Bent's volume on woodpeckers in his *Life Histories of North American Birds* to find out. This is the way to educate yourself. "Every good book," said

Goethe, "can be understood only by him who has something of his own to contribute. He who knows something finds infinitely more." In addition to looking up what I can about some specific bird, I like to keep gathering information on bird and animal behavior in general, information that I might be able to put to use later. It has been said many times that we see with what is behind our eyes rather that what is in front of them. I read to stimulate my mind and get ideas that may help in finding out how birds and animals live.

Although I used to find professional journals informative, I find almost nothing that I can use in the chart- and table-studded articles on behavior in the leading journals of today. Reliance in these articles seems to be on statistics and methodology rather than on prolonged and careful observation in the field. Lesser and more local journals, however, still have notes and articles that can be helpful to anyone trying to work out life histories of common birds.

I have also stocked my library with a variety of books on insects, plants, amphibians, and other fields of natural history. Wide interests, even though one has only a smattering of knowledge, can be useful, as when I was able to read up on the blister beetles in relation to the sweeping of White-breasted Nuthatches or on the coccid that feeds on paper birches in connection with the winter foraging of Downy Woodpeckers.

It is fun to study things. But years of classroom education can kill the best that is in us. The antidote is to take one's education into one's own hands. The "higher education so much needed today," said Sir William Osler, one of the greatest figures in medicine, "is not given in the school, is not to be bought in the market place, but it has to be wrought in each of us for himself."

When I was growing up I loved to read books about birds and other animals. The first books that thrilled me, when I first began to read, were those of Thornton W. Burgess: *Reddy Fox, Johnny Chuck*, and the like. There were over twenty in the series, and I made many trips to the public library to read them. Silly, childish books, one might say, but I do not think so. They depicted wild animals as I loved them and still like to think of them, as fellow creatures that I can talk to, not as beings altogether different from ourselves.

As a freelance amateur, watching birds and other animals because I enjoy doing so, I feel that I can link esthetic, humanistic, and scientific values without loss of face. If I wish to have observations published in *The Wilson Bulletin*, I write in a scientific style, but when I write in general terms, as in this book, I stress that watching birds and animals can be more than just a scientific exercise. Spending hours in quiet, beautiful places can provide a return to health and sanity, and so can having some wild animal or bird that you have hand-raised and cared for as a pet. Jane and I have raised many kinds of birds and animals: beaver, porcupine, raccoons, Belted Kingfishers, and Blue Jays, among others. But regulations are strict today, and keeping wildlife of almost any kind is illegal. In this situation I have found, from my reading, a number of ways you can have wild birds in the home, even keeping some of them, and learn a lot about behavior without breaking any regulations. I have not collected these cases idly. One way to never run out of things to do is to keep collecting, from books and articles by others, things you might like to try someday. If someday I become less able to travel about, these are some of things that I should like to try.

Pine Siskins are extraordinarily tame naturally. Many were coming to our yard in Bethesda in April 1953. Having read that they would come into a bedroom, I put peanut hearts on the outside and inside of our window-sill. It did not take the siskins long to find them. I threw the window open at night and pulled down a Venetian blind. With the blind down, I thought, the siskins won't come until we are awake. No such luck. They came early and made so much noise coming through the slats of the blind and flitting about the room that they woke us up. My experiment was a success and could have developed further except that Jane had three small children to look after, and so the time was not propitious. In the meantime I found reading E. R.

Davis' account of how siskins came to his bedroom an enjoyable substitute. Since siskins liked to wake him up in the morning, he contrived a number of experiments:

I placed a small box of seeds on the window-sill near the head of my bed and over it a glass cover. The next morning one of the birds came and looked through the cover at the food, but, of course, was unable to reach it. After hopping around it and trying in vain to get the food, he came to my pillow and pulled my hair to awaken me. Then he flew to the window and tried to get the seeds again. Failing, he returned to me, pulled my hair and pinched my ear, then went again to the glass-covered box. Three times he did the same, and then I "awoke" and reached for the box. Immediately he scuttled out on my arm and waited until I removed the cover, when he hopped into the box and enjoyed a well-earned breakfast. And that was no accident, for I had the pleasure of seeing the same performance staged many times afterward.

As I said before it was almost impossible for me to enjoy a nap after sunrise. If I just closed my eyes for a moment or two, down would come some member of the flock and pull my hair, pinch my ear, or tweak my nose. Or if that treatment failed to awaken me, he would reach over and gingerly take hold of my eyelid and pull my eye open, for he knew that if I was awakened he would surely get the much desired ration of seeds, and he did. Now and then I would try to fool them. Turning from the window, I made a little tunnel of the bed clothes, some 6–8 inches in length, reaching from my face to the outside so that I could breathe. A few minutes later the search was on and I could hear the birds hopping about the bed clothes. In a little while one of them had discovered the outside opening of the tunnel. Hanging by his claws he bent down and peered into the opening; in the dim light he could see a portion of my face. Hopping down he commenced exploring. First he advanced an inch or two, then beat a hasty retreat. Immediately trying again, he advanced a little farther. About the third or fourth time he succeeded in reaching my face and giving the end of my nose a good nip. This had the desired effect, for I immediately threw back the clothes and he followed my hand to the window where I uncovered the food and he proceeded to devour it. After that the jig was up, and soon it seemed that every member of the flock had become expert tunnel explorers.

Davis performed other experiments, all indicating that Pine Siskins are intelligent. He had empathy. He was obviously sensitive to what was going on in the minds of his visitors. Anyone could have a wonderful time playing around with siskins as Davis did. When I think of all the tortured, complicated, and expensive experiments on animal intelligence that have been performed in laboratories, mostly with dubious results, I reflect on how much easier, simpler, and seemingly more meaningful were Davis' experiments with his free-living birds. He did not go very far, and I think you could have a lot of fun carrying on from where he left off.

An even more remarkable account of birds coming into a house is Len Howard's *Birds as Individuals*. It is impossible to quote her many accounts of the birds that flew in and out of her cottage in Sussex, but she has this to say of the way she began:

> Perhaps it is because of my intense love for birds that they come to me quickly and I have not found any difficulty in gaining their confidence. Directly I moved into Bird Cottage I put up a bird table and bath close to the french window, and a Robin, Blue Tit and Blackbird came at once, many more species, including the Great Tit soon following. I have always talked to my birds in a normal speaking voice, for they soon learn to understand something of speech by its tone. Very quickly this great intimacy developed and the numbers rapidly increased. Besides loving their company, I find immense interest in studying their individual characters and through this close intercourse I can reach a better understanding of their minds.

Howard stresses the inhibiting effect of fear on the birds she observed.

> I have no doubt the Blue Tits and Robins would not have behaved intelligently if they had feared my presence. Often bird behavior is judged when the bird panicked with fear of the watcher. But many humans would prefer not to have an intelligence test when they or their young are in probable danger of immediate death. I find the normal thing is for birds, especially for Tits, to act intelligently in unusual circumstances, unless they get flustered through fear.

It was three months after her cottage had been built that Howard had the following remarkable experience:

> I was busy within, near an open door, when a Blue Tit came fluttering up with cries of distress. She hovered agitatedly close in front of me, her eyes fixed on mine, crying as I had never heard a Blue Tit cry before; it was at once obvious something was wrong and she was asking for my help. Her mate was with her but perched just outside, watching me intently. Directly I went out she stopped crying and they led me to their nesting-box. . . . The whole of her nest had been pulled into fragments . . . and her twelve eggs lay scattered over the hard wooden floor. . . . The lid was shut so it appeared a cat had clawed out the nest in pieces through the entrance hole.
>
> Both tits waited close by, silently watching while I quickly gathered the fragments of nest from the ground, removed the eggs and reformed the nest in the box as well as I could, then replaced the eggs on the right side of the box, thinking she would like it as near as possible the same as before. Directly I had finished the mother bird flew in, and after removing her eggs to the other side of the rather large box, brooded her clutch again. Ten days later the eggs hatched, and she brought off her brood in spite of the calamity because she had sensibly thought of appealing to me for help. What else except thought could have made her

act thus? It is not a bird's instinct to seek man but avoid him over anything in connection with nesting affairs. I had not been long in my cottage and no other bird had been helped over nesting difficulties or anything else. I had merely fed the birds and watched unseen while they built their nests. But many birds had grown tame and they trusted me.

I often think what immense pleasure some people could derive from taming birds that come to their feeders and thus get to know them more closely, as Len Howard did. She seems to have been one of those very special people whom animals and birds trust with little hesitation. It is interesting that Julian Huxley, a biologist with a broad background and humanist inclinations, wrote forewords for Howard's *Birds as Individuals*, as well as for Clare Kipps' *Clarence: The Life of a Sparrow*. Huxley presumably recognized the value of those books. How much valuable work by talented amateurs gets lost because there is no biologist of Huxley's stature around to give it the recognition it deserves? Donald R. Griffin's book *Animal Thinking* is a courageous attempt to get professionals away from their almost medieval notion that man and animals are separate creations with only man having feeling, awareness, and the ability to think. But almost all of the material he uses in making his points is drawn from work by professionals. Nowhere in Griffin's book, which I value highly, have I run across any more impressive example of animal thinking than Len Howard's account of the Blue Tit.

Clarence: the Life of a Sparrow, by Clare Kipps, is one of the gems of bird literature.

This is the story, not of a pet but of an intimate friendship, extending over many years, between a human being and a bird. As I am a widow, living in solitude and comparative seclusion, perhaps no sparrow has ever been privileged to enjoy (or to endure) such exclusive human companionship, and it may throw light on the habits, temperament and possibilities of one of the most interesting and adaptable of all birds.

"The height of wisdom is to see the miraculous in the common," wrote Ralph Waldo Emerson, and this is what Kipps did with her sparrow. It was during the height of the blitz that Kipps, coming home to her bungalow after a long day's duty as an air-raid warden, found a tiny newly hatched, naked, blind, goggle-eyed, and apparently lifeless bird on her doorstep. She fed it with a dropper, as best she could, and, not expecting it to live, wrapped it in flannel and put it in a cupboard for the night.

To my astonishment, early the next morning I heard a faint, continuous sound coming from that airing cupboard—an incredibly thin yet happy sound, the kind of a noise a pin would make if it could sing; and there was the little creature, still in his porcelain cradle, but warm, alert and calling for his breakfast.

Thus began thirteen years of friendship with a Domestic Sparrow, and a record of observations interesting to the last in the ways the sparrow adapted to the infirmities of old age. Kipps was a musician, and no passages of her book are more surprising than those in which she describes the sparrow accompanying her playing on the piano.

He never sang so well as in the early morning and, as I played faster and faster, and higher and higher in the treble, he would pour out his soul in an ecstasy as great, if not as melodious, as any skylark.

One of the great experiences a behavior watcher can have is to raise some bird by hand and, giving it a maximum of freedom, get to know the companionship that can exist between a bird and man. Birds can exhibit many characteristics under these conditions that one would never suspect from seeing them in the wild. Even the smallest of them can exhibit mental traits surprisingly like our own. Hard-nosed scientists almost always dismiss as "anthropomorphism" any talk of birds and other animals' being anything but mechanical robots. But how many of them have ever lived with a wild animal or bird in the manner of Konrad

Lorenz or Clare Kipps? Why should it be regarded as scientific to deny man's relationship with other creatures or to deny that they, too, may be capable of acting intelligently?

The first close view Jane and I ever had of a Starling was on the night of a severe blizzard in Boston. We were living on Beacon Hill, in the center of the city, when my father called out that some sort of bird had come down the chimney, out through the fireplace, and into his room. What we found was a Starling perched on his bedstead and looking much at home. I took the bird to our room on the top floor, where it again perched composedly, as though coming two flights down a chimney into a warm room on a stormy night was no new experience. The next morning we woke up in time to see the bird shake itself, fly to an open window, note that the storm was over, and fly off about its business. There was no doubt in our mind but that Starlings must be smart birds.

Konrad Lorenz recommends Starlings as pets, giving instructions on how to raise and feed one. He called the Starling "the poor man's friend" because it costs nothing to acquire. But I think the appellation a bit demeaning. A British lady, who helped me at a crucial stage in my hornbill watching in Africa, told me that she, as an avid aviculturist, had purchased birds from all over the world. Her favorite was not one she had purchased but a hand-raised Starling. My career as a bird lover is far from over, and I hope some day to raise a Starling, a House Sparrow, or both. M. S. Corbo and D. M. Barras' book *Arnie the Darling Starling* gives an idea of what an attractive companion a Starling can be about a house.

It sometimes surprises me to hear young professional or other ornithologists speak with scorn of any reference that is at all old. I myself tend toward the reverse assumption, finding at times more substance, individuality, and inventiveness in older authors than in modern ones. Gilbert White, one of the first of behavior watchers, made observations on House Martins and other birds in his English garden more than two hundred years ago. "From reading White's *Selborne*," wrote Charles Darwin in his *Autobiography*, "I took much pleasure in watching the habits of birds, and even made notes on the subject. In my simplicity, I remember wondering why every gentleman did not become an ornithologist." Among the pioneers in behavior watching in America is Althea R. Sherman, whose *Birds of an Iowa Dooryard* is a classic of its kind and holds up a model of how resourceful and inventive an amateur can be. Miss Sherman, a woman of very independent character, lived with her sister, a physician, in the old family homestead. The place was surrounded by an acre of abandoned farmland and was ideal for studying birds. In addition to being a born scientist and observer, Althea had an ability to draw and an ability to write. Her studies of the nest life of flickers, House Wrens, Catbirds, phoebes, Kestrels, Screech Owls, and others that came to her yard make informative reading for anyone studying these birds today. And they also reveal how use of imagination and inventiveness can aid in making observations. One of Althea Sherman's ingenious contrivances was a tower with a wooden chimney for observing Chimney Swifts. She was among the first to observe that these birds, in raising their young, are sometimes aided by a third swift, a discovery she made years before the phenomenon of cooperative breeding became generally recognized.

The advantages to studying bird behavior in your own yard, especially in studying nesting, are considerable. You can be at hand at all times of day and, by arranging nest boxes, you can increase your chances of having something to observe. I was surprised, in watching the nesting of a pair of House Wrens for several hours a day one summer, to learn how much went on in our yard that I wasn't aware of. Behavior watching is cumulative. Once you get the knack of it, the more you see and reflect, the more you are apt to observe. And reading, creative reading of the kind that generates ideas and sparks enthusiasm, can be a great asset if you want to keep right on learning through old age.

FIVE

WATCHING BIRDS IN CENTRAL AMERICA

JANE AND I have visited various places in Panama, Costa Rica, and Guatemala that we hoped would be favorable for watching woodpeckers. Places that did not work out as I had hoped did, nonetheless, provide interesting watching. One of these was Palo Verde, located in the center of a huge cattle ranch twenty miles from the main road in Guanacaste province, Costa Rica. When we left for Costa Rica in the winter of 1978, blizzards were paralyzing New York and Boston. But at Palo Verde, in the Pacific lowlands, it was 108 degrees in the shade, with a landscape of volcanic stones, barrel cacti, and low, largely leafless trees—all in a burning sun. I have never felt so close to heat stroke as on our first days there.

This was before I learned to cope, with what for me was a rigorous environment. Was I, a New Englander, soft in fleeing to the tropics? "It is for man the seasons and all their fruits exist," wrote Thoreau in an anthropocentric mood. "The winter was made to concentrate and harden and mature the kernel of his brain, to give tone and firmness and consistency to his thought." This is good, old, rock-bound Puritanism, but we found the northeast was not the only place to have severe conditions that try the spirit. "Devil's Island," Jane called Palo Verde, as she tried to cope with chiggers. If I had had the compensation of seeing more birds and wildlife on my first strolls there I would have felt better, but most of my walks about the ranch house, run by the Organization of Tropical Studies, were surprisingly bleak.

I think these initial difficulties made what we found later the more enjoyable. Adaptation made the difference. Whereas at home walking makes me feel better, at Palo Verde it made me feel worse. And, *mirabile dictu*, the less I walked about, the more I saw. So Jane and I found ourselves sitting out under trees, on our folding chairs, day after day, within one hundred yards or less of the ranch house. The abundance of things to watch and the uniqueness of the place then flooded in on us. In addition to tropical dry forest, Palo Verde includes a vast marsh. The marsh is the remains of a lake that forms with the rains, then slowly dries up the rest of the year. As a harvest of observations swelled my journal and sketches filled Jane's notebook, the heat, the chiggers, and the crowding of the bunkhouse, while never quite forgotten, came to fill a smaller place in our thoughts.

I started my days at Palo Verde by taking a flashlight, while stars were still out, and walking the dirt road that skirted the marsh. The flashlight was for Pauraques. These are Whip-poor-will-like birds that rest on bare earth as a taking-off place from which to pursue passing insects. Their eyes gleam in the dark. When I found one, it usually bobbed up and down making loud *quoit, quoit* vocalizations. The *quoit*s increased in volume, ending in a *whee-ee* as the bird flew off. These vocalizations, especially when mixed with the roars of howler monkeys, made a lively chorus which reached its height at dawn.

As the sun lightened the east, it tinted the undersides of clouds lying motionless above the marsh. It was then that I waded out to a volcanic rock surrounded by croaking frogs. The rock had a round depression where I sat to watch marsh birds come to life. My arrival usually frightened a flock of Blue-winged Teal and Black-bellied Tree-Ducks, part of the thousands of wildfowl that took wing farther out.

The first birds to appear, once I had settled down, were jacanas, birds with long legs and toes for walking on marsh vegetation. As the jacanas emerged from a reed bed, they moved over what looked like a grassy meadow. The grass was actually a floating mass a foot deep, covering the water.

First to appear among the jacanas was an adult, presumably a male, with four half-grown chicks. Jacanas are polyandrous— meaning that one female, remarkably, keeps two to three males busy. She supplies each with eggs, and they do the incubating and raise the young. Young jacanas are largely white, even as juveniles. The parents, in contrast, are dark red-brown with bright yellow bills and frontal shields.

As the jacanas moved into their pasture, Great Egrets and both Tricolored and Little Blue Herons began to arrive, and I saw that each was territorial in driving away others of its kind. The bird on the marsh that excited me most was a solidly built heron with dark, vermiculated plumage—a Bare-throated Tiger-Heron. While the other herons went about stalking prey, the Tiger-Heron perched on a post. What, I wondered, did it feed on? The bird bent low to examine the marsh with neck swelled to nearly the width of its body, then splashed into the water to catch a huge fish, eight inches long with a thick, wide body. The heron, making no effort to subdue its prey, flew back to its post, the fish in its bill. There it perched with head sinking lower and lower as if the fish was too heavy, then dropped it back into the marsh. The oversized fish was as far as I got in learning about the food habits of Tiger-Herons.

A few mornings later a second Tiger-Heron came to a post a little farther along. The first one raised itself straight up, its feathers again moving out until its neck looked remarkably thick and heavy. Then its head sank into its shoulders. Was this the heron's way of saying hello to its mate, or of threatening an enemy? The two met later in water belly deep. Then, with bills pointing in opposite directions, they intertwined necks. I took this behavior to be amatory but, as with the other herons, I wished I could have learned more. With the sun rising, I headed back to the bunkhouse.

A dry wind was sweeping over the ranch at Palo Verde by the time breakfast was over, and the sun was hot. I like miscellaneous watching, and I always looked forward to my visits to the marsh at dawn. But in any place I visit, I also like to find something I can watch at length. How could I accomplish this at

Palo Verde when I was so reluctant to walk about in the heat of the day? Again I thought of Descartes' injunction to do what is simplest and easiest. This was obviously to unfold our chairs under the shade trees by the house and watch from there. We had not been sitting long before I found a pair of Common Caracaras building a nest at the top of a tree almost overhead. Here were exciting birds to watch. Why look farther?

Caracaras are long-legged hawks belonging to the falcon family. With their black crests, white throats and breasts, and white, dark-tipped tails, they are striking birds, whether in flight, when they soar with wings straight out like eagles, or walking on the ground. Their yellow beaks, set in red skin and tipped with blue, are strong and eaglelike. The fact that they eat carrion has been overstressed, for they can also catch live prey.

My first look at the caracaras was on January 8, when I found two of them resting side by side. One was slightly smaller than the other. I found later that this was the male. When his mate put her head down, he nibbled her feathers, and when he lowered his head, she nibbled him, a form of mutual endearment known as *allopreening*. The routines of the two varied little from day to day. They spent much time within a hundred yards of the bunkhouse perching on large limbs of trees overlooking the marsh. This made them easy to find. The female, like many female hawks in the early breeding season, was not very active. She rested most of the time unless she was carrying sticks to the nest, while her mate did the hunting and brought her food. It was a spectacular sight to see him soar and circle over the marsh. He usually flew far out, then dipped behind trees where I could not see how he found his prey. He was generally on his way back in ten minutes to half an hour with a partially plucked bird in his talons. Whether he found the birds dead or injured or caught them on the wing, I had no way of telling.

The male caracara landed, on returning, on a horizontal limb to pluck and tear his prey still further. Among items I picked up on the ground below were the heads of Blue-winged Teal and one jacana. His mate sometimes flew over to him, walked along the limb, and took part or all of his prey away from him. One morning he walked over and gave her a carcass. Then, while she was holding it in her bill, he jumped onto her back in an incomplete mating. On other days he moved close to her after finishing a meal and, with the two almost touching, preened her head and neck; then she did the same for him.

. On walking some distance along the road into the ranch one day, I found a caracara working on the remains of a prehensile-tailed porcupine. The remains were so hard, dry, and skimpy that I wondered why the caracara wasted its time on such a piece of debris. Yet three days later I found it pulling at the same remains again. From these glimpses I decided that the pair by the ranch house, with the male's flights over the marsh, must have been faring pretty well.

In interludes when the caracaras were elsewhere, Jane and I became interested in the holes in trees about us. Every tree seemed to be a center of activity for a creature of some kind, of which iguanas and pygmy-owls were the most conspicuous.

When out looking for Pauraques at dawn, I heard constant *bing, bing, bing*s coming at a rate of 160 a minute. It took some days to discover that the *bing*s were made by a tiny owl, difficult to locate amid leafy branches. Sometimes two of these Ferruginous Pygmy-Owls joined in a duet. The Pygmies continued their *bing, bing*s as the sun rose but, being ventriloquists, they remained difficult to locate. One of them, however, provided us with an interesting spectacle.

It was midmorning when we noticed the little owl flying to a knothole pursued by a large hummingbird. When the owl came to rest, the hummingbird hovered nearby. Was it mobbing the owl? We had no way of telling. The owl glanced about with its quick, sharp, yellow eyes, twitching its tail from side to side as well as up and down.

Its next flight was to a hole that a male Hoffman's Woodpecker, a woodpecker much like our Red-bellied, had been excavating. I knew something would happen then, and it did. The Hoffman's struck the owl like a bullet; there were muffled screechings; and the two fell grappling to the ground. Only the woodpecker flew up. After some moments the pygmy-owl flew to the woods, low over the grass. The woodpecker had vanquished an owl nearly its own size.

The other creatures coming in and out of holes in the grove by the ranch house were mostly iguanas. Iguanas make wonderful watching, but in most Latin American countries the only ones you see are ones hung up in the market place, for they are easy to kill and good to eat. At Palo Verde, however, where they were protected, I was amazed at how plentiful and conspicuous these dinosaurlike creatures were.

The tree most used by the caracaras, the one with the large limb where they plucked their prey, was dominated by the largest of the iguanas. He was a thick-bodied male nearly three feet long with all the array of crests, spines, and armor that a male iguana can have. When he went up a tree, what I took to be the females and smaller males ran down or up other branches. Such readjustments led to much head-bobbing. Big Male threw his head way back, until it pointed upward, then brought it back abruptly, and kept on doing so as if to say, "Scram, you guys, and stay where you belong." When Big Male came down his tree head first on his way for a quick scoot to another tree, his flail-like tail arched over his back and dropped ahead of him in a curve. The tree he ran to, armored with knobbly spines from base to highest limbs and belonging to a family known as the *Bombacaceae*, looked as if it, too, belonged to the age of reptiles. The knobs probably have protective value of some kind, but they made little difference to Big Male.

After spending part of his days in other trees, Big Male always returned to the caracara's tree to spend the night in a hollow limb with several entrances. He sometimes put his head out from one, sometimes another, when he first looked out in the morning. His rising time was when the sun was well up and birds had been active for hours. In spite of his late start, Big Male was seldom in a hurry. With head out and just one leg protruding, he viewed his sunny domain for some time before making a move.

When he finally left the tree, several smaller iguanas, as though held back by Big Male's presence, crawled out from the same hollow. I got the impression that almost every available hollow in trees about the ranch house was the abode of one or more of these reptiles. I was puzzled to know what they ate. We did see one small iguana feed on two occasions, each on small pealike flowers of a leguminous tree. The iguana went out to the end of shaky limbs to eat them. But he did not persist. Little Orange-fronted Parrakeets, feeding on the same flowers, ate a good many more.

I later asked an expert about the feeding habits of iguanas. All he could tell me was that being cold-blooded, iguanas required little to eat. How a creature could have cold blood in an ambient temperature of 108 degrees Fahrenheit was not clear to me. But then I was far from successful at solving all the problems that Jane and I met with in remote places, particularly in Central America. What we did find, however, is that it is fun to go to a new place and discover things about birds and wildlife we hardly knew existed.

When traveling in Central America in winter in the 1970s, Jane and I sought places where we could live reasonably and see wildlife from the doorstep or in unspoiled forest close at hand. The nearest we came to our El Dorado, and a place we visited three times, was Tikal, in Guatemala. I had generally found Lineated Woodpeckers, which are much like our Pileateds, a shy species and difficult to watch in Central American rain forests. But at Tikal, by the Mayan ruins, I found several nests that were ideal for watching. A pair of Lineateds that nested by Temple 2 was so habituated to people that they paid little attention us. We climbed to the plaza every morning early, carrying box breakfasts so that we could watch at the best hours of the day. It was always exciting when the sun first struck the ruins. Few people came before 10:00, and we had the the plaza, the temples, and the Lineateds more or less to ourselves before then.

Temple 2 at one end of the plaza, and the Jaguar Temple at

the other, rise stepwise and clifflike. The birds that dominated the ruins, for those who had an eye for them, were a pair of Orange-breasted Falcons. One could almost always see one on a dead limb rising above the southwest corner of the plaza by Temple 2.

Busy watching the Lineateds, I was slow to realize what an unusual opportunity I was missing with the falcons. Two things about them slowly dawned on me. One was that I could climb the ruined temples to where I could watch them at thirty feet and another, that these falcons were rare in Central America and, until recently, had almost never been studied. But it was not until February 8, 1978, that I was roused to turn aside, for a time, from the Lineateds. This was when the male Orange-breasted, the tiercel, giving cries and with a rush of wings, landed right above me. He was bearing a robin-sized bird in his talons, and small feathers were soon floating in the wind as he plucked it. The falcon was so beautiful that I felt I must climb for a closer look. When I arrived at the top of the temple I was able to see the falcon within thirty feet and at his own level.

The view from the top was magnificent. Ruins of temples lay in one direction, the forest canopy in others. The tiercel continued plucking his prey for twenty minutes, then, giving single cries, flew with it over the plaza and back. He rested a few moments with the prey in his bill, then flew to his mate perched on a tree above where I sat. She had been waiting for him with feathers ruffed. She took the nearly plucked carcass from him and, holding it in one foot, tore into it with quick pulls of her hooked bill. The view of these two beautiful birds at close range was unforgettable. At only twenty feet, they filled the whole field of my binoculars. I could scarcely have been closer. The feet and bill of the male glistened with the blood and juices of his victim.

I now slid into an alcove shaded from the sun to watch the female. Downy feathers clung to her bill as she continued to feed. The prey was small, but it took many nibbles to consume. What a magnificent bird she was! Although the male Orange-breasted Falcon is a third smaller than the female, both have the same plumage—blue-black above, with bright rufous breasts merging into white throats.

The female took wing after fifteen minutes, making the plaza resound with shrill *ca-ca-ca*s that synchronized with her wing-beats. She never went far on her flights. Like falcons of other species at the time of egg-laying, she spent much time on only a few perches, letting her mate bring food to her.

On the following morning the female falcon began giving *chup* calls, crouching flat with head down and wings out as her mate flew to her. He then mounted, giving loud cries as mating took place. The more I watched, the more amazed I was by how noisy the falcons were. Once attuned to their cries, I was continually aware of them, even when they were at a distance.

There is no accounting for tastes. During our three visits to Tikal hundreds of birders went through on Audubon bird tours, checking off species under guidance of a leader. None that passed seemed interested in looking at any bird at any length. Those birders that we talked to regarded it as queer that we should spend two or three weeks a year at what to us was a naturalist's paradise, when it was well known in their circles that one could "do" Tikal in a few days.

It was while watching miscellaneous birds at Tikal that Jane and I saw four Crested Guans, large, dark-colored game birds, come to an open limb at eye level and only thirty feet away. They had hardly landed when they exploded in four directions. What had happenend?

Jane had seen a hawk fly among them. All I knew was that one of the guans was screaming bloody murder. The sounds were mingled with growls. Could the guan have been caught by an ocelot or jaguar? Excited, yet fearful that I might be seen and spoil everything, I crept along the edge of the plateau we were on, hoping to catch a glimpse. I found that the guan making the screams was unharmed. The same bird was also making the growls. My jaguar was a fantasy. The guan suddenly flew toward

me into the center of a tree with the hawk in pursuit. The hawk, stopped by the tree's outer branches, clung with wings beating and tail outspread. I could now see that it was an Ornate Hawk-Eagle.

The guan switched to *cawk, cawk, cawk* notes at a rate of 144 a minute as soon as the hawk left. Then, with crest raised and the red dewlap of its throat showing, it began to preen.

How account for the wild outburst of vocalizations? Much has been written about the alarm calls of birds. Some think that the caller is exposing itself for the good of its fellows. This noble idea kindled my thinking on the guans, not because I agreed with it, but because I saw things differently. Predators, it seems to me, succeed by coming upon their prey unawares. Imagine the effect, then, of the guans, a prey species, breaking into a barrage of screams and growls that are among the loudest and most dramatic sounds one is likely to hear in neotropical forests. Only the howls of howler monkeys are more formidable. Might not such an outburst disconcert a predator such as an Ornate Hawk-Eagle—enough, at any rate, to make it fumble an attack?

There was another element to the guan's outburst that might also have had an effect. The jaguarlike growls fooled me. Might they not also have fooled the hawk-eagle, at least momentarily? I can well imagine the hawk-eagle thinking, "Could there be a big cat in there? Might it not be better to clear out?"

Rails, of kinds I am familiar with in the north, live among reeds and, being nocturnal, are difficult to see. This was true of the comparatively large Gray-necked Wood-Rails we found when we first went to Tikal. Even if I rose at dawn, all I saw of them by the *aguadas*, or small reservoirs, was a glimpse of one disappearing for the day. The next year, however, the wood-rails were staying out for several hours, and by our third year, having become accustomed to the number of people passing by the *aguadas* daily, they were as tame as domestic fowl, five of them running over the lawns that surrounded the reed beds. Here, with the lawns enabling me to move about, was an unusual opportunity for watching an unusual bird. Sitting in one place, then another, I found the wood-rails, with plumages so smooth as to appear almost featherless, beautiful birds to watch. Their pattern of colors—bright rufous on their bodies, blue-gray necks, and jet black under rear ends and tails, plus yellow bills and sturdy red legs—were striking at close range.

The rails fed largely on pond snails. But one afternoon one of them caught a water snake about a foot long and ran away with it writhing in its bill as two other rails pursued. The captor had to keep running to retain its prize. Once at a distance, it put the snake down, rained blows on it, picked it up, shook it, and pounded some more. But the snake was a tough one and seemed to be unsubduable. It was still able to rise, open its mouth, and face its tormentor after twenty-five minutes. If the rail had no appetite to begin with, it must have had one by the time it made its first attempt at swallowing the snake ten minutes later. This first attempt got the snake halfway down—but not for long. With more writhing the snake gained its freedom, only to receive more blows, shakings, and poundings. The rail tried to swallow the snake five more times without success. Then on a seventh attempt, the snake disappeard head first down the rail's gullet, leaving only a few inches of tail hanging out. Downing these last few inches was a hard go. But finally, after a total of forty-five minutes of wrangling, the snake disappeared within the wood-rail. Would the rail now take a rest? Contrary to expectations, and looking as though nothing unusual had happened, the wood-rail resumed looking for pond snails.

The reason I was able to watch this normally shy bird so long and in such detail was its tameness. Wherever I travel I always regard tame or relatively tame "wild" birds as bonanzas for watching. The opportunity of watching such shy birds as Gray-necked Wood-Rails might be hard to duplicate. I could imagine going to Tikal just to study them alone. What an *embarras de richesse* was there! I not only enjoyed my wood-rails but found out later that neither snakes nor pond snails had been described in their diets. They may have found other food as well. I watched them enter a Guatemalan hut one morning and, jumping up on the table, poke around among the cups and dishes.

When I came to the *aguadas* at Tikal at daybreak looking for the wood-rails, I sometimes noted a shift between the night-loving Boat-billed Herons and such day birds as a Green Heron, several Little Blue Herons, two Cattle Egrets, and a dozen or more Melodious Blackbirds. An Anhinga and a pair of Limpkins that roosted in a huge ceiba tree above the *aguadas* started their day by gliding down to a series of piles. The Anhinga took its time about leaving the roost. It was a handsome bird with a soft, fawn-colored neck, upper breast, and back contrasting with the dark of the rest of its body. Whether perching with wings outspread, flying with graceful wingbeats followed by easy glides, or swimming with its snakelike head moving among water weeds, it was a bird worth watching. I had seen Anhingas in the southern states but had never had a chance to watch one closely. The bird at the *aguadas*, being used to people, gave me the opportunity I wanted.

The Anhinga spent much time perching on a bank. I had to wait awhile before it entered the water in a smooth leap, then rested with its longish tail fanned and its body nearly under. This resting was, I think, to get its plumage soaked and free of air bubbles before submerging. Forty-five seconds after it dived, the Anhinga's snakelike head appeared above the surface with a bluish sunfish, four inches long, impaled on the two prongs of its slightly opened bill. I wondered how the bird could get the fish unpronged, grasped, and swallowed. But the Anhinga had no trouble. It jerked its head up and down, and the loosened fish fell between its mandibles.

The Anhinga later swam to a plank and landed on it with an easy leap. Here, only twelve feet from me, it began the process of drying its plumage. I wished that I might have benefited from the fanning. The Anhinga swung its wings back and forth at a rate of 108 times a minute, with its tail going up and down in unison. After eight minutes it flew to an accustomed perch in a bed of reeds to rest during the noon hour.

I witnessed the wing-and-tail fanning a number of times and thought that since Anhingas are common in the American south, wing-and-tail fanning must be well known. No point in writing it up. Then a year later I came across a note by Ann Francis in *The Auk* on "Wing-and-tail flappings in Anhingas: a possible method for drying in the absence of sun." My observations corroborated the author's almost exactly. I was astonished to learn from her article that so striking a habit had never been reported.

Out beyond what we called the "Indian Village" at Tikal lay a long, lonely track, barely a road, that ran to the distant ruins of Uaxatun. The road was at its wildest when Jane and I took walks there on late afternoons. Some distance out there was a muddy stretch with pools of water in deeper ruts. This was hardly a place where you would expect to see one of the more beautiful sights among birds. Yet it was to these dark pools, we found, that a Purple-crowned Fairy, a large and beautiful hummingbird, came to bathe at the approach of evening.

The water in one of the pools was settled and clear one evening when a Purple-crowned Fairy hovered above the water at the closest range of our field glasses. Held upright and almost stationary by its rapidly beating wings, it faced one direction, then another, as if to assure itself that all was safe. I could see, in these moments, every detail of its plumage, from bright purple crown with jet black through the eye, to snow-white belly, long outer tail feathers, and green-gold on the back. After a minute of hovering, the hummer plunged vertically into the pool, sending up splashes of water with each plunge. It was an exquisite ballet, played in the last rays of the sun.

Jane and I continued to walk along the track in the gathering dusk. We soon became aware of strange grunting noises that seemed to be all about us. With what creatures were we surrounded? Suddenly a group of about twenty peccaries, all massed together, came out on the road ahead of us. I could not see them well. Could they be white-lipped peccaries, a frightening thought, as white-lippeds have been known to chase hunters up trees and keep them there all night. I soon saw, to my relief, that the peccaries had the bands of lighter bristles around the neck of collared peccaries. It was a bit scary, nonetheless, to find ourselves in the midst of a herd of them chomping in thickets all around us in the dusk.

Night comes on rapidly in the tropics. We had to walk fast, right on through the peccaries, to get back while we could still see our way. It was in the last fading light that we heard Great Tinamous, a bird somewhat like a small guinea fowl (although no relation), answering one another in the forest. Their haunting, flutelike notes are among the more beautiful ones to be heard in the neotropics. By this time we had reached the Indian Village and were close to the *cabana* where we stayed.

One of the many attractions to behavior watching is that it ties you to a place long enough to let you really get the feel of it. And one way to get such a feel, as we found on the lonely road to Uaxatun, is to be out as night comes on.

SEA BEACH AND SALT MARSH

BY AVOIDING POPULAR birding places and planning our own expeditions, Jane and I have found beautiful places where we could watch birds in our own way. None was better, in the years we went there, than Sapelo, a sea island off the coast of Georgia. It offered a chance to study Pileated Woodpeckers under favorable circumstances, combined with outlooks on miles of unspoiled sea beach and salt marsh where we seldom met anyone. At Sapelo, in the 1970s, we stayed at the Marine Institute of the University of Georgia. The institute is located on a beautiful estate once owned by the Reynolds family of the Reynolds Tobacco Company. Dartmouth College took biology students there for classes in spring. Although I had no official reason for being allowed to go to Sapelo, the institute kindly allowed Jane and me to make repeated visits in early spring to study woodpeckers and other birds, and they provided quarters where we could stay.

Watching Royal Terns, as with so many of my continuing observations, began by chance. Royals are among the most conspicuous and spectacular of the birds at Sapelo, whether hovering above the waves, diving with a splash, or resting somewhere along the beaches in groups of twenty to two hundred or more at the water edge. Here, with orange-red bills and black-topped heads all facing to the wind, the terns made a handsome sight. I had only glanced at these flocks for some years during the 1970s.

In mid-April 1979, however, I found myself curious to know if there were any Caspians among them. Caspian Terns are the same size as Royals but have blood-red bills. I unfolded my chair and began to inspect. Not a Caspian could I find. But in looking for one thing, as often happens, I discovered something else. The terns were carrying on courtship.

I had been interested in the courtship of birds for a long time but had never expected to have an opportunity to watch courting terns. Terns generally nest on islands and, without a boat, the chances of my watching them seemed remote. Royal Terns have never nested on large islands like Sapelo, as far as I know, and it seems unlikely that they ever will. They require spoil banks or reefs, free from trees and predators. What I had discovered at Sapelo was that they can do their courting in one place and their nesting in another.

The copulatory behavior of these terns is most bizarre. It was so striking a feature of the groups that we could commonly see three or four pairs engaged or displaying at the same time. Activities usually began when a male, with neck extended and partially folded wings held out like a skirt, tried to walk around a female. She, meanwhile, kept turning, the effect being like a minuet. The male, with head held high, looked down at her along his orange-red bill. When she paused, he mounted.

The copulations of most birds are brief affairs, a matter of seconds. But not with Royal Terns. Once standing on his mate's shoulders, his lordship seemed content to stay there, looking out to sea over the heads of the other terns. Several times in the course of the next two to four minutes, however, he moved to her rear and then, holding on with his tarsi and beating with his wings, he swerved his tail under hers.

Feeding of females by males in courtship is common to many avian species. Some of the males we watched among the Royals were continually filling the air with *kur-witt, kur-it* calls as they left the flock to return after a while with a fish held crosswise in their bills. The task was then to find their waiting mates. A male I watched found his readily, for she had pushed through to the edge of the crowd. In proffering his fish, the male drew himself up with head high and wings out in the same display as for copulations. She responded with a similar display, then seized his offering.

The males almost always brought in plump fish about three inches long. The females had, it seemed, a definite idea of what they wanted, and anything smaller was rejected. Was this a way, I wondered, of training a mate for his job as provider when chicks arrived?

Watching seabirds can be very different from watching birds on land. As seabirds live completely in the open, one has little trouble following them, and if they live in colonies, no trouble finding nests. Feeling my dearth of experience in watching sea- and shorebirds, I kept an eye open for other birds that I could watch by the sea, particularly large and spectacular ones like the Royals. As things turned out, I did not have far to look.

Jane and I were sitting on top of one of the taller dunes back from the beach one morning, looking out to sea at the spectacle of Brown Pelicans, cormorants, and Royal Terns resting on sandbars along with thousands of shorebirds, when I became excited by the sight of two pairs of oystercatchers in the rough sandy stretch between dunes and beach. They were flying fast in noisy combats with each other. "Eureka," I cried, "Here we have them. They obviously have territories and are about to nest." What luck! We had stumbled on a grandstand seat for watching the breeding behavior of birds that I had long wanted to study. The bold pattern of black heads and necks and gleaming white underparts of the oystercatchers made them stand out across the sands. It was only on closer view that the remaining upperparts appeared gray-brown. Closer views endeared the oystercatchers to us. With their long, red bills and bright red around the eyes, they were droll to look at. Add to these features their solid, chunky shape and sturdy whitish legs and one has a very hand- some bird.

The battles of the territorial pairs of oystercatchers were daily, almost hourly affairs. On our first day the two birds of the south pair suddenly began loud *tweedle, tweedle*s followed by rapid *deedle, deedle, deedle*s as they ran togather, bowing heads up and down. A moment later they were off in a direct flight over the sand toward the north pair, which had invaded their domain. Theirs was no peaceful mission. The southerners came in low over the enemy like a pair of black-and-white fighter-bombers. After several swoops, they flew back the way they had come.

The enemy met the strafing by staying close and flinging themselves on the sand. Once the fighters had passed, they quickly recovered and ran about with heads and bills pointed toward the sand, shoulders hunched and tails depressed as they made their loud cries. They looked as if they were pouring out their indignation.

Hardly had the southerners landed back in their own territory then one of the north pair, making *tweedle* calls in his turn, took wing to deliver a return attack. This time it was the southerners that sprawled on the sand. I could not tell whether the lone attacker was a male, for the sexes of oystercatchers look alike. But I suspected it was, and later observations revealed that the partner staying behind was the female.

Watching the oystercatchers, there were stretches when little seemed to happen. Then, suddenly, something unexpected would turn up. One of the north pair was resting on the upper beach one afternoon when its mate ran a few steps, then flung itself on the sand. It was typical evasive behavior, only there was no enemy in sight. The oystercatcher got up and continued walking down the beach, flinging itself on the sand five more times before reaching the water. What odd behavior. What could it mean?

My hunch was that the daily and often hourly fights between the oystercatchers were emotional experiences. Fighting was much on their minds. The evasive behavior *in vacuo* may, therefore, have been a kind of play or practicing, done when the birds had nothing much else to do. When pondering the problem I was struck by a passage in Peter Matthiessen's book *The Wind Birds*. Speaking of the single-wing display of the Buff-breasted

Sandpiper, Matthiessen wrote that the bird sometimes "displays in perfect solitude, in silence, as if practicing for some dread fray which awaits it in the future."

Whenever I saw the two oystercatchers of a pair run to join each other in the face of an attack, I thought of Robert Ardrey's remark that "outer enmity brings inner amity." There is nothing, in other words, like defense of a territory to strengthen a pair bond.

In only a few days after our watchings began, Jane and I began to see copulations between the south pair of oystercatchers. The female tilted her tail and body, then waited. The male might take a minute or two to reach her, but once mounted, he fell to the right as his tail slid under hers, she holding the tilt position to the end.

Most of the matings we saw involved the south pair. A suspicion that the north pair might be through copulating and already nesting was confirmed on April 16. It was at the start of another glorious day of cloudless skies. The south pair had flown off to some other part of the island to feed, and I turned to concentrate on the lone oystercatcher of the north pair. I guessed that she was the female. She simply stood still for ten minutes. Then I remembered that she had stood by the same place the day before. Could it be her nest scrape? She seemed nervous, for her head and body bobbed up and down. After a seemingly long interval she walked slowly to where a small accumulation of straws and a few stalks of beach grass made a slight elevation. She poked in and around it with her long, red bill. Then, plunking down on her upper breast and raising her body at an angle of forty-five degrees, she began kicking with her legs to make a slight hollow. Could she be laying an egg?

I became excited and wished she would leave so that I could have a look without disturbing her. She flew off after fifteen minutes only to return and watch from not far away. Would she ever give me a chance? Finally, to my joy, she took off on a long flight, and I was free to have a look.

I hurried over the 150 yards of sand between me and the spot where the female had scraped. Keeping my bearings was not easy, for one part of the sands looked much like another. When within twenty feet of the approximate place, I stopped. Looking through my binoculars I was lucky to see two brown eggs covered with irregular black blotches. I did not need to go any closer. Two days later I found three eggs, the full complement for oystercatchers. I suppose I was simple-minded in becoming excited by the oystercatcher's eggs, but I have always taken the discovery of a nest and eggs, ones that I have never seen before, to be a high point in behavior watching. There was, furthermore, more to our watchings than just the striking birds and their activities. Beyond was the constant motion of the tides, the sight of Brown Pelicans diving or resting on sandbars, and the hundreds of cormorants and Royal Terns—a beautiful landscape as a setting for making discoveries.

It was easy to watch Willets when Jane and I were studying oystercatchers at the south end of Sapelo in a following year. One Willet rested on the same piles of cord grass not far from us every morning. It occasionally left to fly high over its territory in the dunes, its wings beating in rapid, shallow flight. On one flight it met a neighbor, and the two glided and flew close together, one diving on the other. The two then returned to their respective territories, our bird alighting on a large sign reading, appropriately, PRIVATE PROPERTY. NO TRESPASSING.

I was puzzled about the nests of the willets. All that oystercatchers do on their breeding territories is easy to see. Once I had learned something of their behavior, I had no difficulty finding their scrapes on open sand. Not so with the Willets. I have read that their nests are easy to find in some coastal areas, but this was not true on the south end of Sapelo.

Leaving Jane to keep track of things by the beach, I walked back and forth among the dunes. What a hopeless enterprise! I skirted dunes; I mounted them; I crisscrossed lower places covered with different kinds of grasses; I walked near and far away from myrtle bushes—all to no avail. After I had walked back and forth thus for a week, my hopes were at a low point, when one morning a Willet flew up from a patch of grass and circled. It stayed close. "It must have a nest here," I thought. I walked over to the grassy area and there, hidden under arching stalks of grass, were four spotted, brown eggs—my first Willet nest.

Sometimes I have stumbled on nests, and sometimes I have had to hunt for them. Those that are the most fun are those that I have found after an arduous search. A hardened expert might say, "A Willet's nest; what of it? The nests are well known, and many people have found them." Fortunately my mind does not work that way. It is the process of hunting and discovering, seeing what birds do with my own eyes, that makes nature alive.

I have never been deterred from studying a bird because others have written a few papers about it: there is just too much to be learned about even our commonest birds. One observer will see a bird from his particular point of view and another from a different angle, the varying approaches all being helpful. Any species of bird, furthermore, needs to be studied under a variety of conditions and in different localities. These considerations guided me when I took to watching herons on Sapelo in 1979. Herons make a good group for watching, whether you are inland or along the coast. Having had little experience with them, I wanted to learn for myself how they might differ in their ways of getting a living. But watching in the salt marshes was not easy, and as usual, I knew that I would get nowhere until I found just the right place. This turned out to be an old boathouse below which ran a tidal creek bordered at low tide by mud flats extending, on the far side, to a jungle of marsh grass.

The variety of herons coming to the creek were a delight to watch. About all that I had seen of them on previous visits was their taking off at a distance, but when I sat quietly, things were different. The three species that ventured close were the Tricolored and Little Blue Herons and the Snowy Egret, all of about the same size. The Little Blue was deliberate about following trickles of water over the mud. All of its poses were graceful. It

frequently stood with head up, looking about with its dark, simple eyes. Then, with head and neck low, it took a few more steps and paused. It was eyeing something in the turbid water and made weaving motions of head, neck, and breast. Was it trying to get a better line on prey not clearly seen? A quick strike and it had a fiddler crab in its bill.

A Snowy Egret that came in view was extremely agile. With white plumes, black bill, and legs with yellow feet, it was like a ballerina always keeping her poise. The egret moved in shallow water with quick little steps, head and neck forward, ready with whirls from side to side and a quick jab for whatever prey might turn up.

My watching of Snowies was not limited to the boathouse. I learned, when driving to the beach, to stop the car on a bridge, using the car for a blind whenever there was something to watch. A Snowy was wading in the incoming tide one afternoon, quick and graceful as usual but seemingly finding nothing. Then it switched to a new activity. First it vibrated one foot back and forth over the bottom, then the other. It was the same movement that I had seen with plover and once with a woodcock—a way of getting worms and other organisms to reveal themselves. Snowy Egrets differ from plover, however, in having black legs and bright yellow feet. One theory, not proven to me, is that the yellow of the Snowy Egret's feet aids in stirring up prey. My hunch, in contrast, is that the yellow provides a light background, aiding in detection of anything passing over its feet in muddy water. So quick is an egret that just a glimpse of a shadowy form might let it strike and seize.

April 13 was one of my best days at the boathouse. The marsh was especially clear and fresh after a rain the day before. I had the misfortune to frighten a Tricolored Heron as I sat down. These slim herons are much too wary. Great was my joy, therefore, when the Tricolored came into view once more. What kind of a show would it put on? It came around the bend of the creek with quick steps, its legs bent so that body, head, and bill were close to the water. A few steps foward, a lightning dart, and some small creature, too small for me to identify, was caught. I saw that the heron could strike in any direction—front, rear, to the sides. The Tricolored was as agile as a lightweight boxer. With a feint here and a strike there, it had its prey baffled. A favorite maneuver was to sneak forward with head and bill tilted to the side and low to the surface, trying, I imagined, to see with the light against the sides of its victim.

It took a while to perceive another maneuver. The Tricolored held its wings slightly out as it moved in its quick, shifty way. Then, running a few steps, it spread its wings, creating a sudden shadow. I had watched Tricoloreds foraging in fresh water but had never seen this. Possibly it would be of less use in waters choked with weeds and algae. Mockingbirds flash their wings on a lawn in the way Tricoloreds do in a tidal creek. The mockingbirds' behavior has been much studied, with great difference of opinion. It is possible that both Mockingbird and Tricolored, by flashing their wings, throw a sudden shadow that startles prey into revealing itself.

Great Blue Herons are among birds that I have found especially difficult to watch. They are shy and, as patient fishermen, they may rest for long periods without doing anything. Such was my usual experience until one day at the boathouse on Sapelo I noticed a Great Blue bending over as though caught by some large object. It raised its head after a minute, and I saw that it had caught a large chunky fish. How could it possibly deal with such a catch? Then, to my surprise, with an upward toss of its head, it downed the huge fish head first. When it flew, the fish sagged as a heavy bulge in its neck.

I had another encounter with a Great Blue by the boathouse on April 12. The tide was halfway down when a bottle-nosed dolphin, looking huge and without much room to maneuver, swam up a side channel. Behind it came a wave traveling along the mud flat. What was it? There was a sudden surge of water as a second dolphin appeared in the swirl. Was it trying to drive fish ashore? A Great Blue Heron flew to the surging water almost instantly, as though it had been following the dolphin. When the dolphin passed up a still smaller creek, the heron followed again. This association of heron and dolphin would have made a first-rate study had I had more weeks on the island. It wasn't until six years later that I found a note by A. P. Ternes on how bottle-nosed dolphins, weighing three to four hundred pounds, push up waves that strand fish on mud flats where they, the dolphins, can catch them. Thus my guess that the dolphins I saw had been doing this was borne out.

Coming from inland, I was always amazed at the number of things there were to watch by sea beach and salt marsh at Sapelo. One could spend years there studying the behavior of birds without exhausting the possibilities. What makes observations possible is finding a really good lookout, as I did with the boathouse.

None of the birds by the boathouse were as tame as a Whimbrel we found there. It seemed to accept us, whether it was asleep with striped head and long, curved bill tucked under a wing, or stalking about on the mud as the tide rose. This was a boon to us, for Whimbrels, at least in my experience, are among the shiest of shorebirds. Other Whimbrels at Sapelo stayed in groups, but ours remained by itself. It flew in one day with another Whimbrel, both calling the wonderful *kur-leoo, kur-leoo, kur-leoo* of their kind, but only our bird landed. Its companion veered away. On another day five Whimbrel came in fast, coasting on bent wings like ducks, as though our bird was a decoy. But the newcomers, on seeing us, kept on going.

It was when the tide was rising over the flats that our curlew became most active, slicing the whole length of its long, curved bill into one fiddler crab burrow after another. Although its bill came up empty most of the time, the Whimbrel drew male fiddlers out of their burrows occasionally and carried them to the water's edge. Here the Whimbrel nibbled at the base of the crab's giant claw until it fell away. Then, swishing the remainder of the crab free of mud, it swallowed its prey whole—a rough, awkward morsel by our standards, but not, it seemed, by the Whimbrel's.

When its legs and bill became coated with glistening mud from probing into tunnels, the Whimbrel walked to the creek to swish them free. As though this was not enough, our bird swung one foot back and forth to get it clean, then used it to clean its bill still further. Now that it was clean and handsome, what would it do? Take a rest? Contrary to expectations, it went after the fiddlers again and was soon as muddy as ever.

A stroke of good fortune that sometimes comes to the watcher is to run across a relatively tame individual of an otherwise shy species. After watching it for a number of days, I came to feel that the Whimbrel was a special friend. Perhaps it was because I was unhurried and watching only one bird, a particularly tame one, that I developed a special awareness of how beautiful the salt marsh was.

So passed many pleasant hours of undisturbed watching from the boathouse on Sapelo. When the tide rose over the flats, the creek became a placid lake. The life of the marsh came to a standstill. Some Willets, the Whimbrel, and a Spotted Sandpiper rested on rafts of dead cord grass. The only bird stirring was a female Northern Harrier gliding low, in hesitant flight over the marsh. She paused to plunk down in several places before coming up with a small rat which she bore to a sandy ridge. Then all was peaceful. The beauty of the place was enough.

SEVEN

SOUTH FLORIDA

BECAUSE OF MY particular interest in the courtship of birds, I found the dances of Crowned Cranes in Africa one of the more beautiful things we watched there. The cranes came to a field near our house in Entebbe, and had I not been studying hornbills, I might have concentrated on them. Twenty-four years later, in 1978, I had the idea that perhaps I could find a substitute for the Crowneds in watching the courtship of Sandhill Cranes in Florida. I called Jim Layne, then director of the Archbold Biological Station, located in Lake Placid, south-central Florida, and found that cranes bred in its vicinity. Thus began one of many watchings that Jane and I carried on in Florida over a number of years.

My first three days of looking for Sandhills were disappointing. I could not find a place that seemed at all suitable. Then I had a break. Only a few miles from the Archbold Station I glimpsed a crane flying. Ahead was a quiet sandy road. I turned the car into it. Not far along was a marshy pond and to one side of it, a pair of Sandhills. One was light gray, the other browner. They were individually marked. But I soon ran into difficulties. The Archbold Station is in cattle country, and I was warned about going through fences. Cattlemen are leery of rustlers and poachers. But I wanted to follow my cranes, so I rolled under a fence that ran along the road. I had not gone far when a car stopped and a man yelled out:

"Hey, what are you doing there?"

"Looking for whoopers," I answered, knowing that all cranes are "whoopers" to natives in Florida.

"Oh," he replied, "I thought you were lookin' for pot planes." At least I was not being taken for a cattle rustler! I met the ranch owner, Mr. Blount, on the following day, and he assured me that I was welcome to come any time. He too was interested in the "whooping cranes," which he said had had young on the place the year before.

The cranes did not do much in the first weeks of February. By hiding behind scattered clumps of saw palmettos, I found it easy to stay within fifty yards or less of them as they fed on roots of grasses. I wanted to find out where they spent the night. I had seen no signs of courtship, but the best time to see courtship in birds is early in the morning. If I could find the cranes' roosting place, I could be at hand at dawn.

Finding a pair feeding by a marsh as the sun went down, I said to myself, "This is their roosting place," and left. The cranes were there, and dusk was coming on; all seemed obvious. But when I arrived the next morning there was not a sign of a crane. Did the cranes feed and fly by night? I wandered all about the usual places, but not a crane could I find. After an hour, still empty-handed, I heard a distant trumpeting. Could that be my birds?

I set off cross-country as fast as I could, rolling under two fences and stampeding two herds of cattle. Beyond lay a marsh I had not seen before, surrounded by pasture, and there beside it was my pair of cranes. The brown one, which later turned out to be the female, pointed her neck and bill forward as if expectant, then jumped into the air, and Light Gray, her mate, followed. I was excited watching the two huge birds flying over the pasture trumpeting *gar-oo, gar-oo*. I was thrilled to have found their roosting marsh.

So far I had found a place where I was able to follow a pair of cranes easily, a pair that were individually marked, and I had found their roosting place. I had had to do some hunting to work these things out, but hunting for something that is not easy to find is exciting. Still, what about the courtship I had come to watch?

I started a routine the following morning that was to go on for some days. Leaving Archbold's at the first streaks of dawn and carrying breakfast in a paper bag, I headed for the cattle pasture with the isolated marsh. Once there I unfolded my chair and sat down to watch. Cattle Egrets and White Ibis started flying by in the cold mist as the sun rose. Then, at 6:50 A.M. or close to it, the cranes walked from their roost marsh into the pasture and spent twenty minutes feeding before flying to Blount's land. This morning flight was usually the only flight I saw during the day. The cranes were walkers, seeming to prefer a long walk to what might have been a short flight, a habit that enabled me to keep up with them.

Things took a different turn on the second day. An immature crane, possibly a young one of the year before, had joined the pair. At this time the parents did something I had not seen. Every so often the female started tossing her head as she made loud *tuck-tuck-tuck*s, while her mate pointed his bill skyward to call *gar-oo, gar-oo, gar-oo*. This was the famed unison call, one of the more striking performances, with variations, of cranes the world over. Sometimes the two birds stood close, at others ten or so feet apart as they proclaimed, or so I thought, "We are a pair, we are together." I had never seen them do this before. It seemed to have taken the presence of another pair trumpeting in the distance, and possibly the arrival of the immature one, to set them off.

The trumpetings of my pair were so loud that the message must have carried for miles. Was there another message also? Were the parents proclaiming to their yearling, "We are about to nest. You must go. You are on your own. You must go."

The two cranes copulated after the yearling left. I now knew for the first time which was the male and which the female. Had I known earlier, I could have learned their sexes from the unison calls. The female always calls *tuck, tuck, tuck* and her mate *gar-oo, gar-oo*.

The matings of the pair of cranes were striking performances. I witnessed one on each of four successive mornings. It was not easy to see all of the details on any one morning, but I was able to see many of them on the morning of February 16. The cranes were feeding along a plowed strip, driving their bills into up-turned sods and scattering them about. Could I get any nearer? A bulldozer was parked nearby. If I could get to it without scaring the cranes, what a place it would make for watching! Getting the dozer between me and the cranes, I sneaked up carefully, then climbed cautiously to the driver's seat. Now I was in the front row. No sooner was I seated than the female held her wings out and crouched as the male came to her. He planted one foot on her right, then one foot on her left shoulder, sinking down with shanks against her back. She continued to hold her great wings out as he waved his to keep balance. Then his tail swung under hers. They separated after eight seconds. But the performance was not over, for the two swung into an odd pose. With necks bent and bills touching the ground, they looked as though their bills and feet were anchored while some force was pulling their necks and bodies upward. The mated cranes held this strange position for several seconds, then resumed feeding.

I witnessed the first dances of my cranes on the day after the copulation. I had seen the male toss bits of debris into the air or take a few steps with wings out on days before this. His mate, however, had not responded. On February 14 both began bowing. The male then burst into a fit of wing-waving, leaping this way and that, throwing his head back, calling, kicking his legs forward, and tossing debris into the air. Sometimes he was close to his mate, sometimes fifteen feet away. She joined in with a few leaps but went on to a special performance of her own—a low running with wings arched over her back and tail fanned.

As with the cranes' copulations, I never saw more than one burst of dancing a day. The most spectacular of these occurred some days later. Jane and I had brought our supper to sit by the pond in the evening. The cranes were feeding quietly, raising their heads every so often to look about. By 6:15 P.M. the day

came to an end as the sun, a great orange orb, sank behind a
screen of pines. The cranes were unaffected for a few minutes.
Then they began bowing. What better than a dance in the
twilight? Waving wings and leaping about, they splashed water
in all directions as well as tossing it into the air. It was a sudden,
wild, and thrilling performance. After it was over, the two
walked to the shore, paused a moment looking westward, then
ran to take wing. With strong downward strokes, they flew over
fields toward their roost marsh, giving loud *gar-oo*s as they went.
I was glad that Jane had had a chance to see them.

There are many kinds of pleasures associated with behavior-
watching. Hunting is one of them. Few of man's ways of earning
a living today are as enjoyable as the hunting way of life that our
ancestors lived for hundreds of thousands of years. Stalking a pair
of Sandhill Cranes, keeping as close as I could without frightening them, and learning of their habits, gave me the feeling of
being a hunter. It was easy to imagine the tall, alert cranes as
being game. Our hunter ancestors, surrounded by a world of
incredible beauty, must have had a feeling for their fellow creatures that lived around them in great numbers, a feeling we
cannot easily imagine. Behavior-watching, when you become
absorbed in what you are doing as I did with the Sandhill Cranes
in Florida, allows you to recapture for a while the kind of one-to-
one relation with nature that our not-too-remote ancestors grew
up knowing.

In reading what I could about Sandhill Cranes, I came upon
the following passage in Herbert Brandt's *Alaskan Bird Trails*.
As Brandt and two Eskimo boys approached a crane's nest in a
kayak, the cranes started dancing. One of the boys drew an arrow
from his quiver, and

> with this he began to beat the tightly drawn sealskin deck
> of the boat so as to produce the only native instrumental
> music. Then both boys chanted their dreamy crane song
> accompanied by rythmic 'tom-tom' beating of their impro-
> vised drum.

As they sang the two great birds continued their dance and seemed to keep perfect time with the strange wild music. When the boys beat the drum and sang faster, the dancers moved more quickly and when the music slowed the birds seemed to do likewise. Their motions were not continuous, but were punctuated by a slight pause at the end of each movement, thus giving them all the grace for which the Spanish minuet dance is noted.

On March 11, I found the pair of Sandhill Cranes by their roosting marsh at dawn. Their behavior had obviously changed. There was no dancing. The female's mind seemed to be on something else. She lifted her bill skyward and called *gar-oo* three times. What was stirring? She finally ran and sprang into the air, with her mate following, to fly north on a long flight. Where could my cranes have gone? They had disappeared over a tract of scrubland, and following as best I could, I found myself at the edge of an extensive marsh, not of lily pads and water hyacinths but of swaying grasses and no open water. Could this be the place where they were going to nest? I looked over the sea of grass but saw no cranes. I tried several vantage points without success. What a disappointment! My watchings of the pair's courtship would be so neatly rounded out if I could only find the nest. Not finding any cranes on a second sweep with my glasses, I left to return on the following morning. There was one spot that might bear some watching. It was where pickerel weed, indicating deeper water, grew. Why not sit and watch from a distance?

At first nothing happened. The marsh was almost barren of life of any kind and singularly quiet. Then after thirty minutes the female crane, hitherto completely hidden, stood up. She must have been standing on her nest to look so conspicuous. She seemed to be arranging her eggs, for she kept her head down.

I felt a strong urge to wade over to check. How exciting to have a look. But I killed the idea. Why should I break into the privacy of my beloved pair? I had always taken care not to frighten them and did not want to do so now. I liked to feel that, after weeks of seeing me around, they had come to regard me as harmless. If I scared them from their nest, they might desert, and our trust would be broken. I stood to learn more by not obtruding.

I spent an hour or two every morning watching by the marsh from a folding chair that I set up in the scrub. I was lucky on most mornings if I saw the female crane stand up to arrange her nest. She spent the night there, but her mate was never in a hurry to relieve her in the morning. I often found him feeding alone in a pond where I had seen the pair feeding when they were together. The male was irregular about the times when he flew to the marsh, and I had to wait an hour or more on several mornings before I saw him come flying in over the scrub. What a huge bird! He always flew straight to the pickerel weed, his mate standing up as he lowered his long legs to land.

The two of the pair were united once more. Standing high, they raised their heads in a loud, ringing unison call. Then the female, wading into the water, moved to fly away as the male settled on the eggs. How long would it be before the long incubation was over? One book said twenty-eight days, but it was thirty-five before I noticed both of the pair standing by the nest, an indication that the eggs had hatched. It was five more days before I glimpsed the chicks out in the marsh.

The several months that I spent with these cranes were among the more memorable I have spent with birds. I had visited them seven days a week, and because I moved carefully so as never to frighten them, I believed that they had come to regard me as not too much of a threat. I loved the birds, and it was thrilling to enter into their lives as much as I did. Quiet watching: what a feeling of the immensity and wonder of nature it can give you!

My observations of the cranes never resulted in a publication, but the experience brought out to me how unimportant that can be. Little happened at the marsh during many of the hours that I spent there. I built a bower for convenience in the shade of a sand pine, raising my folding armchair on a platform of logs so that I could see over the tops of the bushes. Then, sitting back in comfort, I let my morning hour or two come to be a time of leisure, of enjoying the white clouds, the blue sky, the soaring of vultures—the simple being alive in a beautiful place. How much I enjoyed going nowhere and doing nothing, but being watchful, just letting things happen. It is at such times that I have a wonderful sense of the peacefulness of nature.

Watching the cranes, I discovered how lovely the Florida scrub can be. I had thought of it as a kind of wasteland left from fires and the cutting off of the pines, and so it is in many places. What I did not realize was that the Florida scrub in its original state, such as it was where I was sitting, is just as much a natural area as sand dunes. It has its indigenous plants, tiny oaks, cacti, and others, spaced out across stretches of white sand. This patch of scrub became my garden and, as I sat in my bower, I thought of the story of a visitor to Wordsworth's house. The visitor wanted to see the poet's study and was shown a book-lined chamber. "That," remarked the housekeeper, "is his library, but his study is outdoors."

When studying the Sandhill Cranes, I usually parked my car by a small, reedy pond that only existed due to continued rains. One cold, windy morning, reluctant to get out and follow the cranes, I sat watching two Great Egrets walk through the pond, then rest by the shore. Neither seemed to find anything to eat. Could the cold have slowed down the aquatic life they fed upon, or did the wind, by roughening the surface, make prey harder to see?

I became more interested when two immature White Ibis alighted by the egrets. All four birds now moved together through the marsh. Eight more ibis flew in as the group came to a stretch of open water. One egret now drove the other away. The attacker acted, I thought, as if it was becoming territorial about its flock of ibis which, with additions flying in, soon increased to thirty-two birds. The egret followed the ibis closely, standing above them like a hen above chicks. When the ibis came close to the car I could see that while many probes of their sickle bills ended in nothing, an occasional foray ended with the capture of a crawfish. I also noted that the egret, while not catching much in some places, struck out in others with its daggerlike bill and long neck at swimming prey—in one place twelve times in ten minutes and in another four times in five.

When the birds had all left after two hours, it was apparent that the association of egret and ibis was not a chance affair but a mutually beneficial one, each species seeking out the other. The ibis, in advancing through the marsh in close formation with heads down probing, benefited the egret by serving as beaters, stirring up aquatic life that the egret was quick to seize. What was the benefit to the ibis? Protection, perhaps. When the ibis were feeding in their usual manner, with heads down like a flock of sheep, they were in a poor position to guard against predators. In this situation the Great Egret, standing tall, alert, and always on the *qui vive*, made an ideal sentinel, on the lookout against any bobcat, fox, or raptor that might try to capture an ibis when its head was down.

In our years of watching in Florida the arrival of Swallow-tailed Kites in spring was always one of the most exciting events. Kites are masters of the air. With snow-white heads and breasts, blue-gray mantels, and easy, graceful flight, they remind me of sea-birds. So expert are they at catching every little updraft that they have few equals in ability to sail wherever they want to go. They live in the air as naturally as other creatures on the ground, catching insects on the wing, or snatching frogs, lizards, or even nestling birds while soaring by outer branches. Kites even feed in the air, pulling at prey held in their talons as they balance with continual tilts of wings and long tails.

A difficulty of studying these birds in the breeding season is that they nest at the tops of tall trees in woods and swamps where, on looking up, one can see almost nothing but masses of branches, vines, and Spanish moss. N. F. Snyder had to construct an elaborate tower in order to study a nesting pair in the Everglades. In seeking birds that I can study my way (that is, with the least effort), I try to find places where Jane and I can watch without a blind and without having to use mechanical devices.

In the case of the kites we found a place only three miles from the Archbold Station that was well suited to our kind of watching. The kites were courting, resting, and preening on dead pines in a field on one side of a road, while building nests at the very tops of pines on the other, all within view of the place where we sat by the roadside. We usually saw the long, slim forms of five kites resting and preening when we arrived at dawn. The birds did much perching at this time. This was especially true of the females, which were awaiting the attentions of their mates, attentions that included copulations and eleven or twelve courtship feedings a morning.

The copulations of one pair of kites were always spectacular. After circling as if to test air currents, the male approached his mate in a long glide from the rear. She, seeing him coming, flattened herself with wings out and head and neck down, the male dropping on her back and letting his tapering wings fall on either side. Matings lasted about thirty seconds, and on some mornings we witnessed up to three of them by a single pair.

The male's foraging included a mixture of soaring and gliding that carried him across a field to woods beyond and never took long. We could see his white-and-gray plumage in the distance as he flapped and turned among leafy treetops until, brushing against a branch, he captured an anole, a small green lizard. He bent his head down to transfer the anole from talons to bill while flying back. His mate flattened, in the same pose as for copulation, on seeing him coming. The male alighted beside her and waited. She then reached over, took the anole from him, and tossed it down.

Things did not always go so smoothly. On March 19 the male kite had copulated three times and fed his mate four times when he returned with a long-legged frog. She refused to take it. He was seemingly nonplussed and circled over the road and field a few times before trying again. But she remained uninterested. What to do? The male kept trying with the frog, twelve times in all, acting the while as if not knowing whether to fly away or to persist.

It was of interest that among the next eighty-four courtship feedings we watched, the offering was an anole about two inches long in eighty-three and an unidentified object in one. The female kite seemed to be very choosy. While other prey might do at other times, in the business of courtship the male was expected to bring one kind of item only, an anole of definite size. We had, curiously, witnessed an almost identical fussiness in female Royal Terns, which at times of copulations would only accept fish of a certain length from their attentive mates.

Two weeks after mating, the female of our pair was sitting on a nest built near the very top of a tall pine. When looking up, I found that the tossing of bird and nest in the wind made me a trifle seasick.

The relatively little used road from which we watched the kites worked out well as a base. We had become so much a part of the landscape by the time we left Florida that children in school buses were calling out, "Buzzard watchers!" as they passed us each morning.

Jane and I drove south from the Archbold Biological Station on the afternoon of March 4, prospecting for a new place to watch birds. It was an unusually warm afternoon, and after an hour with no success, we started back. Huge areas of central Florida have often seemed so desolate. We felt we had been wasting our time. Then suddenly, out of nowhere, we came upon a dramatic sight. Thousands of Tree Swallows were clustering in three tall bayberry bushes by the roadside. They were packed in like a swarm of bees with many hanging upside down. There were almost no berries on the bushes, and it was easy to see that the swallows were not feeding. After less than a minute, the swallows poured out with a rush of wings and dispersed.

The sky was getting darker. A storm was brewing. We had not driven two hundred yards before we saw the swallows piling into tall bayberries again. Then out they came, before they had even settled. I got out of the car to watch. The swallows were now gathering in a great vortex that acted like a magnet in pulling more swallows from all points of the compass. Once together, they soared *en masse* with almost no beating of wings. The center of the vortex was nearly over my head and, as the lowest swallows were only twenty feet up, the sky seemed filled with their bodies. It was like looking into the eye of a hurricane against a background of dark clouds and thunder. I ran for the car as raindrops began to fall. Once inside I noticed that the swallows had dropped low in a dark mass that rose and fell, extended and shortened, as it moved over the tops of low trees and disappeared. The preroosting displays that we had watched were, I think, precipitated by the transient darkness produced by the rain squalls.

A point difficult for a behavior watcher to learn, as I have found to my regret more than once, is not to pass up a good opportunity for observation, whether by a roadside or elsewhere. A good opportunity for watching may never recur. Had there been a number of people in our car, Jane and I might never have stopped. We seized the opportunity, but what did the behavior of the swallows mean? Witmer Stone noted that wintering Tree Swallows may congregate on bushes lacking berries or even leaves, but he gave no explanation. I was unable, at first, to find any plausible one myself. In such situations it helps, if possible, to observe the unaccountable phenomenon again. When Jane and I were at one end of Sapelo Island a month later, we ran across a flock of possibly ten thousand Tree Swallows. A few rain squalls swept over the island, and each time the sky darkened, the swallows alighted on the beach or on bayberry bushes. This time I had an idea. I had recently talked with Peter Ward of the studies he and A. Zahavi had made of Red-billed Quealeas in Africa. These birds congregate in a huge communal roosts. The question in Ward's mind was why the quealeas should travel great distances, at a considerable expense of time and energy, to do so. What were the survival advantages? His theory was that the roosts serve as information centers. If one group of quealeas do poorly in foraging one day they can, by flying to a roost, attach themselves to some other group the next day, a group that, by their behavior, seem to know where they are going.

Birds such as quealeas, starlings, and parrakeets that use large roosts have preroosting displays advertising their location. It seemed to me that the idea might apply to the Tree Swallows. They winter farther north than other hirundines, feeding on wax myrtle berries and flying insects, resources that are patchy in winter. If due to cold, wind, or other factors, one group of swallows does poorly one day, it can, by joining a large roost, be led to more productive areas the next.

Since school days I had wanted to see more Red-shouldered Hawks. Their screaming over the March woods is one of the most stirring bird sounds in New England. In studying woodpeckers, I was often in lowlands where Red-shouldereds nested, but because of the wooded nature of the country, I was never able to see much of their courtship. Florida did not seem much better for hawks until I found the Hendrie cattle ranch in 1980. Situated eleven miles down the road from the Archbold Station, the ranch was an ideal place for watching Red-shouldereds. Like many of the Florida race, a pair we found by a swamp were relatively tame. Another boon was that the male and female could be distinguished individually, the female having the light, whitish breast typical of the Florida race and the male, identified at times of copulations, having the reddish breast typical of northern Red-shouldereds.

As our watchings developed, it was neither the matings, the steep dives of the male over the nest site, nor the circlings and screamings of the pair that provided the most excitement. On one particular morning, as on others when Jane and I went to the ranch, she had walked one way, the way that appealed to her, while I had wandered about looking for things I wanted to follow. I doubt if any two people can be equally interested in the same things at exactly the same time, and that is why Jane and I have often done our watching separately wherever we have traveled, feeling that, to have the relation with nature and wildlife that we like to have, one must be alone. How can one concentrate otherwise? A further advantage to walking about separately is that we generally have a lot to tell each other when we meet. And so it was on this morning when, having set out on my own, I saw three hawks soaring above the swamp. One lowered its talons as it dove on a second one and nearly struck it. It then climbed and dove again. The next thing I saw, before they passed out of my sight, were two hawks whirling toward the ground with talons locked. At this moment Jane, from her side of the swamp, saw the same hawks dropping toward a spot in an open pasture only ten yards from where she stood. Using 8 x 30 binoculars she could see that each Red-shouldered was grasping a talon of the other, with the other leg hanging free. The two, with wings partly spread, whirled slowly earthward. When within a foot of the ground, one shook its talons to break loose. The combatants then separated and rose upward as one pursued the other in soaring flight to the east, well beyond the usual range of the pair.

The female had meanwhile landed in a leafless tree near Jane, to be joined by her mate five minutes later. Two days earlier we had watched the female giving short cries before, during, and after two copulations. Now she gave the same cries on the leafless tree in series of three to five every fifteen to twenty seconds for a half-hour, but her mate made no response. Thus in a piece of cooperative watching from different points, Jane and I were able to witness the whole of a most interesting event of which we would otherwise have seen only a piece.

I had tried for several years to find a long-term project to replace my woodpecker studies, having fun in the meanwhile watching birds of various other kinds. While watching the Red-shouldered Hawks at the Hendrie ranch one bleak winter day, I was led to a crow bowing deeply, then making an odd-sounding *cu-koo*. That crow changed my life.

It is surprising to me sometimes how things that I have long wanted to happen eventually do. One of the great events of my childhood, when I had an insatiable desire for pets, was when a policeman handed me a fledgling crow that he had picked up on the sidewalk where we lived. The crow arrived just as we were leaving for our country place in New Hampshire. I gave Joe, my crow, his freedom in the country, and he stayed around all summer as part of the family until he flew away in September. Since then I have had a lifelong love of crows. It thus seemed miraculous that I should have stumbled on a paradise for crows at the Hendrie ranch. No place in North America could have been more ideal for studying crows in my style. Mr. Hendrie had been feeding and protecting wildlife for over twenty-five years, and the crows were remarkably tame.

What I found, beginning in 1981, was that in spite of its being among the commonest of birds, almost nothing was known about some of the main features of the life of the American Crow. There had been amazingly little study by researchers. Within a few months of starting our studies, I was excited to find that the crows I was watching lived in territorial groups and were cooperative breeders. The helpers, sometimes up to six or seven of them, aided in all phases of nesting, from nest building to feeding the incubating female and, after hatching, feeding the young before and after they fledged.

I found many other things about the crows, about their courtship and copulatory behavior and about the dominance of the breeding males and the low, uncrowlike vocalizations they sometimes made. I also witnessed crows' versatility in foraging and storing food while nesting. It seemed almost incredible that there was practically nothing in the literature about these facets of their lives. With the crows so tame, and made tamer by my feeding them every day, we found lots to discover in the five years during which we spent the months from January to May at the Hendrie ranch.

Each year, after being away for eight months, I would drive the two miles or more into the center of the ranch wondering whether our crows would still be there. Would they remember us? Parked in my usual place, I would get out of the car and look for our crows. Not a one in sight. "Here, Crowsy," I would call, "corn, Crowsy, corn." Immediately Jane and I would hear *caws* from various directions as the crows came flying in. It was always as though we had never been away.

When I scattered corn, I fed each group of crows within its own territory. Viewing them thus from twenty to twenty-five feet every morning enabled me to get to know them well. The crows did not get all the corn. Wild pigs with litters, razor-backs, were common on the ranch when we first went there, and litters of four to six piglets, after feeding on corn, might fall on their sides to rest. As many as three crows might then perch on an exposed flank or by walking around, search for lice on the piglets. They seemed to find the grooming of piglets profitable for, once established, a crow might peck one at rates of sixty times a minute. The piglets appeared to enjoy the attention, for they solicited it by rolling over and did not mind when a crow stood on a head or pulled a leg aside. The crows groomed the range cattle as well, the cows soliciting attention by putting their tails out to give the crows a place to perch when attending to their rear ends where the lice were located.

It was the low *cu-koo* vocalization that first attracted me to the crows. What did it mean? Jane and I, when close to crows, heard it hundreds of times in our years at the ranch without being able to attach any one meaning. We did notice, however, that when a crow seemed to want to communicate something to us, that was the vocalization it used. I was crossing a wide stretch of pasture one morning with not a crow in sight when suddenly out of nowhere I heard a *cu-koo*. Turning, I found that five crows had alighted behind me silently. They were thickly bunched and pecking rapidly as if feeding on corn. But there was no corn there, nor anything else to feed on. I recognized that they were informing me by pantomine of what they wanted. I had never fed them out in the middle of the wide pasture. I had, however, walked by their usual feeding place at the edge of a wood that morning without feeding them.

Is it unusual for an animal of one species to convey its thoughts to one of another species? I do not think so. The piglets let the crows know that they wanted to be groomed by rolling over in front of them. The cows conveyed the same message by holding out their tails. To the crows, I think, Jane and I were just one more kind of animal on the ranch, providing corn instead of lice, to be solicited in a way that was equally clear.

During our last months at the ranch I was particularly struck by how friendly some of the birds and other animals seemed to have become. The year before, Wild Turkeys, that had come to feed on the corn that I put out, started to drive the crows away. I had to keep the turkeys from coming. But curiously, a year after our contretemps, I had several indications that the turkeys were still friendly even though I no longer fed them. I was sitting in an open pasture one morning when I saw four gobblers walking along a stream bank one hundred yards away. One detached itself from the others and walked all the way over to stand three feet in front of where I sat. There, with neck upstretched, it looked me in the face at eye level, then walked back to join the others.

An even odder experience happened a month later. I was sitting in woods at the edge of a swamp watching some fledgling crows when a hen turkey suddenly ran up to within about three feet of me to seize a black snake, a black racer, by the back of the neck. She held the snake in her beak for a few moments, then dropped it before returning to her downy chicks or poults, which she led to within nine feet of me. I got up and followed her as she made her way along the edge of the swamp, neither she nor her chicks seeming to mind. This is the way I am happiest with wildlife, when it is tame, confiding, unafraid. I have no explanations for the turkeys' behavior except that when Jane and I raised a number of domestic turkeys one summer, we were amazed at what personable, knowing birds they were. Perhaps this experience gave me empathy with the Wild Turkeys. Friendliness is a two-way business. Perhaps the Wild Turkeys sensed that I understood them. At least I like to think so.

Other creatures I enjoyed at the Hendrie ranch during our years of crow watching were alligators, again with some prior background. When I entered Harvard as a freshman in 1928, a friend sent me an eight-inch alligator from Florida. Oscar, as I called him, went through four years of college with me, occupying a large aquarium in my room and adding a touch of wildness. I took him to New Hampshire every April to liberate him in a small pond. There he throve as he never did in his academic setting. If I went to visit him in July or August, I would usually find him dozing on the far bank. If I tossed bits of bread into the water, Oscar, wide awake in a flash, would leap into the water and, lashing with his tail, come over at full speed to dive, turn, and twist after the minnows attracted by the bread. It was only when the water got cold in September that I could catch Oscar again and return him to Cambridge.

How I longed, having seen Oscar as his real self in summer in New England, to visit a place in the south where I could watch wild alligators. A misapprehension that I and many others had for a long time was that alligators and crocodiles were essentially ferocious creatures without attractive attributes such as caring for their offspring. It came as a surprise, therefore, to learn in my reading that mother and even father crocodiles and alligators can be solicitous about both eggs and young. I was anxious to discover a place for observing such things myself.

The Hendrie ranch gave me the opportunity I wanted when, in 1985, our last year there, fourteen little Oscars climbed out on the edge of a water hole every morning to sun themselves on a grassy bank. They were soon followed by their mother, about seven feet long and, to one side, by a male three feet longer. The family were in these positions on April 18 when a Great Blue Heron landed and started walking toward them as I watched. I had suspected for some time that Great Blues preyed on young 'gators, and I watched with interest. The female alligator rose up on her forelegs and rushed at the heron with jaws open. The heron was not much disturbed. It turned to walk around the end of the water hole, wading slowly as it fed along the water edge.

The mother alligator returned to her young, then slipped down the bank with head pointed toward the heron as she disappeared under water. The heron seemed to sense what she was up to, for it now stood motionless looking in her direction. I stood motionless also, camera in hand, only thirty feet farther along the shore. Both heron and alligator were used to my being around. Nothing happened for several minutes. The water remained undisturbed. Then suddenly the 'gator leapt from beneath the surface with jaws open, and the heron, as my photograph later showed, fled toward open pasture with its wings out and drooping. The alligator did not come very close, and I think that she was mainly trying to frighten the heron away from her young.

The general indifference of wildlife to us after our five years at the Hendrie ranch was very pleasing to Jane and me. It made us feel as though, having moved into a new neighborhood, we had finally become as accepted as any cow or horse. This is the kind of milieu I love for watching. If I did not band the crows or frighten them by climbing to their nests, it was not because I loved science the less, but because I loved trying to understand undisturbed nature the more. Only when wild animals go about their business paying little attention to me do I feel I get an idea of what wonderful creatures they are. The ranch offered a not-to-be-forgotten combination of the wild and the tame. Our years there were a fitting climax to our years watching wildlife in the south in the simplest ways possible.

EIGHT

CHANCE AND THE PREPARED MIND

DISCOVERIES DO NOT have to be big to give pleasure. The beginner can find the same kind of joy in observation as someone who has been watching all his life. After forty years I still enjoy small things I note about birds that live in the yard or on a farm across the road. I have come to feel from working in two fields of biology, viruses and birds, that discovery is more an art than a science, an art in which principles holding for one field can work equally well for another. As an undergraduate at Harvard I took a course with the philosopher Alfred North Whitehead. The only work required was to write an essay on "connexity." The word is not in the dictionary, and Whitehead offered no explanations. Every student had to decide what it meant for himself. To me "connexity" meant tying things together, seeing relationships between different fields, breaking down the walls between departments. Were I required to write an essay on "connexity" today, I would write it on the relation of discovery to chance in history, science, natural history, and other fields.

When Abraham Lincoln was running a store in Illinois, a man came by in a covered wagon headed west. He sold Lincoln a barrel that Lincoln didn't want but bought for half a dollar just to oblige. On emptying rubbish out of the barrel later, Lincoln found a book at the bottom—*Blackstone's Commentaries on the Laws of England*. Thus "by accident, by a stroke of luck," as Carl Sandburg narrates the story, Lincoln became "owner of the one famous book that young men then studying law had to read first

of all; it had sneaked into his hands without his expecting it."
One of my favorite epigrams, to the same effect, is Pasteur's
"Chance favors the prepared mind." Lincoln was prepared for his
discovery.

Nowhere in the history of science is mental preparation better
illustrated than in Alexander Fleming's discovery of penicillin.
In looking over his bacteriological plates one morning he found
one of them contaminated. Any ordinary bacteriologist would
have thrown it away, but Fleming, as André Maurois wrote in
his biography of the scientist, "had for a long time been hunting
for a substance which should be able to kill the pathogenic
microbes without damage to the patient. Pure chance deposited
this substance on his bench. . . . Had he not been waiting for
fifteen years, he would not have recognized the unknown visitor
for what it was."

Over and again in this book I stress how observations stumbled on by chance, ones I could not have anticipated, have
provided the best opportunities for getting to know birds and
other wildlife. It was a crow calling *cu-koo* that started me on
seven years of studying crows. It was some odd noises outside our
bedroom window that started me on ten months of watching
Black and White Casqued Hornbills in Africa. Ideas arise from
work, but once one begins to have ideas, the gods intervene and
chance is able to operate.

It has also struck me that some of my discoveries have come
when I felt despondent. This was true on the cold, gray day in
Florida when I heard a crow calling *cu-koo*. Part of the fun of
reading the history of science is finding that what one thought a
personal idiosyncrasy has been the experience of others as well.
Jane Goodall wrote the following about her first really exciting
discovery on chimpanzees in Africa: "That morning I felt despondent, for I had trudged the mountains for hours and had
seen no chimpanzees at all. Then, as I headed for the Peak, I
spotted a black shape beside the red earth mound of a termite
nest." What she found was a chimpanzee using a tool, a modified
blade of saw grass, to spear and pull termites out of the mound.

Another example of despondency prior to discovery is that of William Morton Wheeler. He was head of the Department of Zoology at the University of Texas when, discouraged by having too much teaching to do and not enough time for research, he happened by a dry stream bed near the campus, where he had gone to eat his lunch. While eating, Wheeler noted a line of ants carrying leaves. After watching them for a while, he said to himself, "These are worth a lifetime of study." With this idea in mind, as Mary and Ensign Evans relate in an article on Wheeler and his work, he went on to become an authority on ants.

With viruses as with birds, I found that chance observations were often the ones leading to my best discoveries. There was much interest in the relation of viruses to cancer when I started doing research at the National Institutes of Health. On looking for a problem on which to work, I became fascinated by an account of sarcomas that develop in rats in an unusual way. Rats have long been known to develop cysts when infected by the larval form of cat tapeworms. The larvae induce cysts in the livers of rats, and the sarcomas develop in the walls of the cysts. In the early 1900s a French scientist, Borrel, suggested that the larvae were carriers of a virus that led to the sarcomas. Proving or disproving Borrel's hypothesis was an offbeat problem no one else was working on. Why not give it a try? Starting with such a problem did not appear easy, but I was fortunate in finding the very collaborator I needed—a parasitologist who happened to be studying cat tapeworms. He was glad to supply me with rats, complete with liver sarcomas and their accompanying larvae. The question was, could a cancer-inducing virus be isolated from the sarcomas or larvae? I tried twelve times with various tissue cultures and, on the twelfth, isolated a virus. It did not induce cancers but did prove to be a new virus, the first to be discovered in a group now known as "parvoviruses."

I became much interested in my parvovirus and, on coming to the Dartmouth Medical School in 1961, I wanted to continue my research. I had had little luck in isolating the virus from rats without cysts, but I had what I thought was a lead. A note written by a pathologist twenty years earlier described little round bodies known as "inclusions" in the nuclei of cells of wild rats. My parvovirus induced similar inclusions. Could the inclusions of the wild rats be due to the virus? To the surprise of my Dartmouth colleagues, who thought of me as an outdoor enthusiast, I began to frequent a burning dump on the outskirts of Lebanon, New Hampshire, just south of Hanover. Rats, moving in and out among the blackened cans and gabarge at the edge of the dump, to the accompaniment of exploding bottles and occasional flames under a pall of acrid blue-gray smoke, proved a fascinating study.

My assistant and I caught many rats. They all had intranuclear inclusions, but not a virus could I find. If the inclusions were not due to my virus, what could have caused them? I am not a great reader of current literature, especially in fields not related to my own, but as luck would have it a friend showed me an article by a German scientist on lead poisoning induced in laboratory rats. In tissue sections of affected rats, *mirabile dictu*, were inclusions exactly like those in the dump rats. My pursuit of dump rats now took on a new dimension. If they did not have my virus, did they have lead poisoning? They certainly did. As I found from blood tests run by the State of New Hampshire, no less that 100 percent of the dump rats had lead poisoning. But did they have cancers?

With more searching I found malignant carcinomas in 5 percent of the dump rats I surveyed. This is a high figure considering that wild rats with cancer probably do not live very long. My observations now became relevant. One of the most effective ways of getting lead poisoning, whether in man or rat, is by inhaling lead from burning trash such as old battery cases or material containing white lead paint. That colorful blue-gray smoke hanging over the Lebanon dump was far from healthy for rats, and people coming to the dump were breathing the same smoke when the wind was right. My findings were published in *The Journal of the National Cancer Institute*. Since city dumps were begining to be closed in New Hampshire around that time, I do not know that my findings had any special impact. Nonetheless they illustrate that while you may not find what you are looking for in research, you may find something as good or better.

When I started out in virology I wondered whether my amateur interest in birds might not cut in on my interest in viruses, which I also found absorbing. I need not have worried. I enjoyed the freedom of my amateur approach to birds so much that I used the same approach when pursuing viruses. As David Lack, who started out as an amateur ornithologist before becoming a professional, wrote, "It is absolutely essential that research should remain a pastime, even if it becomes a profession."

A question I have wondered about is what manner of men were the great discoverers. Were they men of broad interests, or were they narrowly oriented? I found, of course, that one cannot make generalizations. I am frankly a hero-worshiper, however, and my inclination, whether in teaching or in research, is toward men of broad interests. George Herbert Palmer, one of the most beloved of Harvard professors in the 1890s, had this to say on the subject: "For developing personal power it is well . . . for each teacher to cultivate interests unconnected with his official work. Let the mathematician turn to the English poets, the teacher of classics to the study of birds and flowers, and each will gain a lightness, a freedom from exhaustion, a mental hospitality."

Charles Nicolle, a French scientist and one of the great discoverers in man's conquest of disease, exhibited some of this lightness and mental hospitality. Typhus fever had been a scourge for centuries when Nicolle went to investigate it in Tunis in 1903. The disease was raging unchecked in poor sections of the city. To visit the poor was highly dangerous; two of Nicolle's associates caught the disease and died. Nicolle, however, continued to visit a Muslim hospital where Arab poor were dying of typhus. It was on one of these visits, as Nicolle described in his *Biologie de l'Invention*, that he passed an emaciated Arab who, bearing all the marks of the affliction, had collapsed at the hospital gates. Once inside the hospital, Nicolle wondered why the poor should catch typhus outside the hospital but never transmit it inside. In a flash of insight he realized that, once inside, patients were washed and their clothing removed. Nicolle concluded that typhus could only be transmitted by an ectoparasite removed with the clothing. There could be no other vector but the louse, the ordinary body louse, "the gray companion of the poor." Nicolle proved his intuition by a series of carefully planned experiments.

Nicolle's discovery was based on a chance observation. Simple, one might say. But as Alfred North Whitehead remarked, "It requires a very unusual mind to undertake the analysis of the obvious."

As a result of delousing programs based on Nicolle's discoveries, untold millions of Europeans were saved from typhus in World War I when the conditions of trench warfare, plus the prevalence of typhus in Russia as well as in North Africa, made it a tremendous threat.

What manner of man was Charles Nicolle, this winner of one of the earliest Nobel Prizes in medicine? What were his interests? According to Hans Zinsser, who worked in Nicolle's laboratory in 1925, "Nicolle was of the stuff of which the French Encyclopaedists were made. I have seen his intellectual scope approached only by a few Frenchmen and an occasional German of the old school—a type of learning that cannot be acquired by study alone, but represents the ripening of gifted minds that are attracted by everything about them worthy of interest." Nicolle began his day at 5:00 A.M., when he wrote his essays (and also a prize-winning novel). His laboratory in Tunis attracted kindred spirits: "Burnet," as Zinsser writes, "distinguished for his studies on Malta fever, was the author of a highly intelligent book of literary criticism. The entomologist was a poet; and one of the assistants a classicist who in his leisure hours was studying Roman archaeology."

Turning again to the lightness that can come from having many interests, I like to think of John Locke (1632–1704), who became in succession a scientist associated with the galaxy of brilliant men who founded the Royal Society; a physician, one of the most respected of his day; a government official who became an expert on trade; and finally the greatest English philosopher of the early eighteenth century, whose ideas had much to do with the development of religious toleration and democratic government.

Yet how light Locke was in spirit! He refers to his *Essay Concerning Human Understanding* as "the diversion of some of my idle and heavy hours. . . . Its searches after truth are a sort of hunting and hawking after ideas, wherein the very pursuit makes a great part of the pleasure. Every step the mind takes in its progress towards knowledge makes some discovery, which is not only new, but best, too, for the time at least." I love Locke's simplicity. I would like to make bird watching, among other things, a hunting and hawking after ideas. And like Nicolle and his associates, I would like also to be attracted to everything about me worthy of interest, even if it be only a burning dump where rats abound.

NINE

THE YEAR AROUND IN NEW HAMPSHIRE

I LOVE NEW HAMPSHIRE winters—the snowy landscapes, the cold, bracing mountain air, the sparkling sunny days. But how barren the woods can be of birdlife! How, I wondered when we first moved to Lyme, can I ever find projects enough to keep me going through winter months? I need not have worried. Hairy, Downy, and Pileated Woodpeckers and White-breasted Nuthatches all begin their breeding behavior in midwinter and, with trees bare of foliage, that is the best time of year to see them. Winter can also be an optimal time for studying roosting, foraging, and other habits.

It was nearly a mile from our house in Lyme to the remains of an old beaver pond which we called Ben's Swamp. I loved the walk into Ben's Swamp in January and February in the late 1960s. Wanting to be at the swamp at dawn, I started when it was still dark with myriads of stars in the sky and temperatures near zero. I had first gone to the swamp to watch Downy and Hairy Woodpeckers emerge from their roost holes and to follow them from there, but soon White-breasted Nuthatches came to attract my attention. The woodpeckers and nuthatches roosted in stubs that rose from the old pond bed. I had found out what a good place Ben's Swamp was for observing when, one morning in late November, two Hairies, five Downies, and one White-breasted Nuthatch emerged from holes at about 6:15 A.M. Would these species interact or compete with each other as winter came on?

On January 3, I came upon a male Downy excavating a roost

hole three feet above the snow and, on later visits, I found him roosting in it. But the stub was rotten. It blew down in February, and the Downy shifted to a birch stub that had been occupied by a nuthatch. Such interchanges added interest to my watchings. After a succession of them I was never sure what bird would emerge from what hole on early mornings. Since White-breasted Nuthatches are about the same size as Downies, I wondered which species was dominant. In two of three interchanges it was the nuthatch that replaced the Downy. Possibly, on the evening before, the former had simply been the one to get to the hole first and occupy it.

Near Ben's Swamp I followed the courtship of a male White-breasted Nuthatch and his mate in near-zero weather when the woods were deep in snow. The male's finest and most prolonged singing was in the first half-hour of the day on mornings from January to March. After leaving his roost in the swamp, he nearly always flew to the topmost branch of an oak. There he remained for varying lengths of time as a lone bird. As though to call his mate, who roosted at a distance, he rested at right angles to his perch, with white breast gleaming in the first rays of the sun, while singing flat-sounding *what, what, what*s in series of eight to ten. These were followed by silent intervals in which the male nuthatch's body swayed slowly from side to side in an arc. When he started singing again his head and neck shot up only to bow lower and lower with each successive note. After two or three minutes of facing in one direction, he hopped around to sing in the opposite.

Five to ten minutes usually passed before the male suddenly changed from dull *what, what*s to musical *wurp, wurp, wurp*s. It was at this time that I heard the first *kun*s or *kun-un*s of his approaching mate. She was usually at a distance and in no hurry. When she finally arrived the male stopped singing, and the two moved off through woods together.

There were more elaborate performances on some mornings. In these the female, perching below and three yards from the male, swayed slowly from side to side, then became motionless as if held by his song. With his back to her in a nearly vertical position, her mate bowed progressively with each far-carrying *wurp*, displaying in succession, "the black of his crown and his rough, raised mane, then the blue-gray of his back, then the variegated pattern of his expanded tail, then—at the end of his bow, a flash of ruddy brown" (A. C. Bent).

Having started with the roosting and courtship of my nuthatch pair in midwinter, I followed them on through the next spring, summer, and fall. Among other behaviors I observed females carrying nest materials into natural cavities in old sugar maples; the bizarre sweeping of nest entrances by males and females; parents and juveniles traveling together in summer; and the caching of acorns and other food during the fall. The watching meant hundreds of hours that brought me to the woods in all seasons, and I enjoyed every hour.

It might seem from parts of this book that behavior-watching is, in the main, a sedentary occupation, the amount of activity involved, however, varies from place to place and from one time of year to another. Jane and I both like exercise, and behavior-watching, when one has to move about a good deal to keep up with nuthatches or other birds in winter, can provide a good deal of it.

The longish walk through winter woods to where I studied the nuthatches and other birds at Ben's Swamp was often an occasion to look for animal tracks in the snow. I did not find much out of the ordinary on most days, but I always liked to know what animals were stirring and where. Conditions for tracking were especially favorable on the morning of March 11. Snow had fallen earlier but had stopped by 10:00 A.M. when I came upon an abundance of fisher tracks. They were of two sizes; one decidedly larger, about four inches in length, which I believed were tracks of a male, and others about half their size, those of a female. The snow was well trampled, and bits of fur suggested that the two had been mating. There were six of these trampled areas extending twenty-five yards from the base of a hollow basswood. The fishers had scrambled up and down the base of the tree, leaving bits of bark on the snow. Looking up I saw a freshly gnawed hole, fifteen feet above the ground. The cavity within was obviously an old one, part of a fissure running up and down the trunk. The gnawings were only superficial. The opening, being about four inches wide by six deep, did not appear large enough for the male to enter, and I wondered if the female might not have selected it for this reason. It would keep her mate from entering and interfering with the young. I continued to visit the basswood without perceiving any signs that the hole was occupied. The snow was granular, however, and not very good for tracking.

Jane was walking in woods nearby on April 7, twenty-seven days after the mating, when she heard what she thought was a porcupine scrambling up a tree. On coming closer, she found that the noises were coming from inside the basswood—a medley of pipings and squeakings that reminded her of suckling ferrets we had once had. As she looked up the mother fisher put her head out. Female fishers have a gestation time (a result of delayed implantation) of nearly a year, so we wondered, in reconstructing events, whether the fisher had not given birth to the present litter in March and then mated again around the same time. My finding a record of the mating on fresh snow was unusual. Our male ferret, when mating, seized the female by the back of the neck with his teeth, and if male fishers have the same habit, it would account for the bits of fur I saw on the snow.

Having to walk a half-hour through woods to a study area can have its advantages, especially if you follow more or less the same route every day. I have noticed a number of times that things casually noted over a number of days can lead to interesting observations later on. I had noted that a large fisher was coming to our woods early in the winter. It then disappeared, but its coming had heightened my interest in fishers and the possibility of seeing one. I like to walk with things in mind that I would like to see. The broader a behavior watcher's interests, the more alive the woods become.

Many ants were going up and down the trunk of a spruce tree from a pile of old boards in our yard on June 20, when I noticed a robin pecking at the base of the spruce, then applying ants to the undersurfaces of its wings with rapid vibratory motions of its head. The contortions made the robin appear very active, for it faced now this way, now that, and often lost its balance. The bird kept the anting up for ten minutes without letup.

I saw a robin sunbathing a month earlier, on May 23. I was searching for a Killdeer nest on a stretch of bare earth across the road from our house when I noted a male robin on the ground not ten feet from me. It was holding its head to one side, as if to catch the sun, and had its bill wide open. The feathers of the robin's head and body were ruffed out, but its wings were closed. The bird held this odd position in seeming indifference to my being so close, as if in a trance. It spied an insect after three minutes and ran to catch it. It then spread out on the ground with belly and extended wings flat to the earth, but quickly after, it resumed a normal position and flew off.

In studying birds and animals it is well to be alert to everything they do, whether it makes sense or not. Anting and sunbathing are certainly puzzling phenomena. The tucking of ants at the bases of wing feathers and the exposure of skin to ultraviolet light are thought to be related to control of feather mites, especially at the time of molting. It has never been clear to me, however, why birds doing it—and many species do—should go into a trancelike state, thus exposing themselves to possible predation. Does the trance in some way affect the physiology of the skin and thus troublesome ectoparasites that may be on it?

I was ambling about woods in Tamworth, where we continued to keep our old house as a summer place after moving to Lyme, at midday on June 26 when a Whip-poor-will flew from the ground and hovered before my face. It then alighted parallel to the limb of a fallen tree four feet above the ground and ten feet from where I stood. The Whip-poor-will was facing me and holding an egg against the bark. Although the bird's feet were not visible, it appeared that the egg was being held with legs and feet. The Whip-poor-will flew away with the egg a minute later.

I then discovered two more eggs lying on dead leaves six to seven feet from where the bird had been perching. One was whole, and a chick had just begun to pierce the shell of the second. The eggs, although shaded, lay adjacent to a bare area exposed to the sun and one hundred feet from a field.

When I returned an hour later, the bird flew up as before, carrying an egg in the region of its legs and hovering before me. It then flew to perch on a log twenty-five feet from the nesting site, still holding the egg. A downy brown chick, making low *bee-rp*s, had by now emerged from its egg on the leaves. When I returned at 2:00 P.M., the Whip-poor-will hovered, then perched crosswise on a limb. It was not carrying an egg. A chick and an egg were at the nesting site. It appeared possible that the bird had lost its third egg when flying away with it. The second chick had hatched by the following morning.

In looking up what I could about Whip-poor-wills I could find no accounts of their or related species' carrying eggs. A number of accounts have been published since, however, of egg carrying by other members of the family, Caprimulgidae or nightjars, to which the Whip-poor-will belongs. Moving eggs to safer places is simplified by these birds' laying their eggs on the ground. When in Karamoja, an arid province in northern Uganda, my son Mike and I discovered a Freckled Nightjar incubating eggs on bare rock on top of a granite boulder. Although I had encountered extraordinary examples of protective coloration among insects, I had never seen protection so complete among birds as that of the Freckled Nightjar when incubating. I could see nothing on the top of the boulder when I stood six feet away. The whole granite surface was homogeneous speckles. Only with careful scrutiny could I make out the outlines of the parent bird. The nightjar's plumage had flecks just like the mottlings of lichens and quartz in the granite. With its eyelids closed and its oddly shaped beak, radiating stiff bristles at its base, the nightjar became further unbirdlike by half-spreading its wings and tail. It would fly away when I came within three feet. The whitish eggs were then obvious on the bare rock. When

I returned on later occasions I studied the boulder from a short distance using field glasses. Bird and eggs were gone. I thought with dismay that I had probably enabled some predator, possibly the Fan-tailed Raven whose nest I had found on a nearby cliff, to swoop down and take the eggs by frightening the nightjar away. Then I would take another look and gradually make out the closed eyelids and bristly bill. The bird had fooled me completely.

One can have surprises in behavior-watching. I was not expecting to make a discovery when I came out onto the shores of a shallow, deserted beaver pond in Lyme early one August. Logs and rocks, once under water, were now exposed. Everything looked bare except for bushes and trees which were starting to grow in. These details were important because, had I not had good views of goldfinches coming to the pond, I might not have appreciated what they were doing. The birds kept coming to the water to dip their bills. Why? They did not seem to be drinking. Picking a female for closer observation, I watched her fly to a snag, bend down, then seize strands of algae and eat them like spaghetti. A male came and did the same. Neither bird made the motions of lifting the head up and down that birds make when drinking. Having found a distinctive piece of behavior to study, I returned on other days. On one of them a female alighted on a log surrounded by black water, bobbed her head up and down as if looking for something, then swallowed seventeen strands of algae (*Spirogyra*) three to four inches long. A goldfinch on August 27 did still better, consuming strands up to ten inches long. These took considerable effort to down, some of the strands catching on her breast and one around her head.

With nesting over and many birds molting or preparing to depart on migration, August can be a comparatively dull month for watching. Goldfinches nest later than other birds, however, and I was pleased to have them provide me with something to watch through the entire month. Accompanying the pleasure a behavior watcher can have in finding something studiable is the added pleasure of hunting through the bird literature and discovering what others have noted. The only pertinent note that I could find on the goldfinches was one by H. G. Digioia who, some years before, had observed goldfinches eating *Spirogyra* in Georgia. The habit thus appeared to be widespread. But why should goldfinches eat algae? I had no idea until I happened on an article by Michael Avery on Sharp-tailed Munias in Malayasia, an article I could have easily missed. These birds, according to Avery, gear their breeding seasons to the availability of rice and algae, algae being a protein-rich food providing important nourishment, especially to birds raising young.

It was at the beginning of September 1953 that I sat down at the top of a wooded slope in Tamworth to look across a stretch of pines. Fall warblers were passing through. Perhaps I could get a better look by sitting in this advantageous place. My attention was soon diverted by a red squirrel scampering about with a pine cone in its mouth pointing forward like a cigar. Red squirrels are such bright, animated creatures that I always enjoy an occasion for watching them, whatever they are doing.

It soon became obvious that six squirrels lived in the area, but only one, Squirrel A, had a territory free of undergrowth and lower tree limbs. I was thus able to observe its entire territory from any one of a number of spots. As the squirrel occasionally ran around the periphery of its territory from one pine trunk to another, its boundaries were fairly definite. All pine cones within the boundaries that had been cut or had fallen naturally were carried toward the center, marked by a pile of stones adjacent to a dry brook bed. The brook divided the territory more or less in half, the territory running 140 feet north and south and 60 feet east and west. Four other squirrels had territories east, west, and north of Squirrel A.

A's activities were usually of the same pattern. It would run around the north end of its territory, which contained most of the pines, and pick up any cones it might find on the ground. Cones were seized at the base, the squirrel holding them pointed forward as it ran over the pine needles. In almost every instance the cones were laid on open ground or in the brook bed close to the rock pile, in clusters of five to eight. At other times the squirrel dug holes in the forest floor at the base of a pine near a bushy field, in a direction where it had no squirrel neighbors, pushing as many as three or four cones into each hole. Some of these cones were already half buried. It seemed that each cone might be deposited, hidden, and finally reburied before the squirrel was satisfied. Although some cones were carried into the stone pile, others were moved by stages from the northern to the southern half of the territory. Every so often Squirrel A paused to give a burst of song, as did its neighbors. These songs, mixtures of sputtery *tcher-r-r* and *tchuk* vocalizations, enabled me to keep track of squirrels that I could not see. Some of the longest songs occurred in the evening.

During my observations, Squirrel A had no encounters with other squirrels. Its neighbor Squirrel B, however, had territorial conflicts with *its* neighbor Squirrel C when it went to the north of its storage area. Squirrel C then chased B around tree trunks and over the ground until B was back where it belonged. The situation then changed, with B chasing C back the way it had come.

Little had been written about any mammal's territorial behavior in the early 1950s, and as I found when I came to write up my observations, no one had described storage territories in red squirrels. The idea of territory was familiar to ornithologists in the early 1950s from Eliot Howard's classic *Territory in Bird Life* but was not so well known to mammalogists. What I had done with the red squirrels, unwittingly, was to watch them as if they were birds. Like birds with territories, they sang songs proclaiming ownership and defended boundaries.

I had been lucky in coming upon the squirrels in a good place for watching. A behavior watcher needs a sense of place. Not all places are suitable. With the squirrels I was sitting on top of a steep bank with a good view down into woods that were free of undergrowth. These assets would have been of little use, however, had I not been watching the squirrels in a year when white pines were bearing a bumper crop of cones. Another point was that there was only one squirrel that I could watch really well, and this simplified observations.

Red-breasted Nuthatches are delightful birds to study. By 1972 I had observed their courtship and nesting both in the wild and with a hand-raised pair in my aviary, but I had had little success in observing them in winter, when they were not always around.

Nineteen seventy-two was a year when the hemlocks in our area were loaded with cones. Hemlock cones mature in October, and by the eighteenth I found both chickadees and Red-breasteds coming to them. It might take a nuthatch two to twelve seconds to extract a seed and then twelve to fifteen seconds to store it in a nearby hardwood or sometimes in the bark of the trunk or larger limbs of the hemlock itself.

The winter was unusually mild. The scales of the hemlock cones, which open only in cold, dry weather, remained closed, and Red-breasted Nuthatches were difficult to find. A light snowfall in early November covered all trees and branches. I found no birds until I came to a grove of hemlocks where flat branches had kept the ground free of snow. Red-breasted Nuthatches and chickadees were foraging here on hemlock seeds that had fallen to the ground. Ground foraging became more pronounced as the season progressed, especially when snow had lain on the ground for some days, and seeds, shaken loose by wind or other agencies, had time to accumulate on the crust. The nuthatches seemed more efficient foragers than the chickadees, for they often picked up a number of seeds at a time before flying to a convenient hard surface which they used as an anvil to pound the seeds against.

Weeks of desultory feeding on hemlocks in November and December ended dramatically when temperatures fell to well below freezing in the second week of January 1973. The scales on the hemlock cones opened wide in the wind, sun, and drier air that arrived with the low temperatures. The chickadees and nuthatches were again attracted to the exposed seeds. When they concentrated on just a few hemlocks, I was sometimes able to watch them for several hours at a time. I encountered two females and a male Red-breasted in one flock, the only time I ever saw more than a pair. The optimal feeding conditions dwindled in less than a week. With a return of milder weather, associations of nuthatches and chickadees became infrequent. Intensely cold weather returned on February 1 and 11, but the supply of hemlock seeds had become exhausted, and I found no more birds of either species visiting the hemlocks.

Red-breasted Nuthatches and chickadees were not the only ones that came to the cones. Red squirrels, being able to gnaw into them at any time, and Pine Siskins, coming in flocks of up to fifty, were by far the biggest users.

Reasons why birds of diverse species associate can differ under different conditions. I think the association of the Red-breasted Nuthatches and chickadees, when they could have fed separately, was a matter of winter survival. The hemlock seeds were available to them only under certain weather conditions. If only a few nuthatches were present, they might feed casually. The presence of chickadees competing for seeds may have incited the nuthatches to store as much as possible while the supply lasted. Bumper crops of seeds of one kind or another provide special opportunities for watching. An aspect of watching the Red-breasteds that fascinated me was the way the hemlock cones closed in warm, damp weather and opened widely when it was cold and dry—an adaptation that possibly ensures a wide dispersal of their vaned seeds.

When making a special study of crows from 1981 to 1987, I ran a winter feeding station for them on the Record farm, across the road from where we live in Lyme, using leftovers from the butcherings of farm animals, or on occasion whole carcasses. I placed or had them dumped on the far end of a field, near woods and about 250 yards from the farm buildings. In its first five years my feeding station was so successful in attracting crows, small numbers of ravens, and other wildlife that I have continued it as a way of having something to watch in winter. The farm buildings are on elevated ground, enabling me to use my car as a watching place on cold, windy, or stormy days.

On October 7, 1987, I had a heifer carcass unloaded sixty feet from the woods. Since crows, ravens, and smaller mammals cannot get through hides that are at all thick, I chopped the heifer open in a number of places with an ax. Nothing came to it. As I had found in the past, crows and ravens can be very wary about approaching anything new.

My feeding station was renewed on October 26 with viscera and scraps from the butchering of two cows. I did not think much of anything would come soon, especially on October 28 when it was raining. But a coyote came from the woods just as I arrived at the farm, fed on the pile for two or three minutes, then returned to the woods with a scrap a foot long. In four minutes it was back to feed again, going up on a rock now and then to look around. Crows, which had not fed on the pile hitherto, came out when the coyote was there, three feeding within six feet of it. The coyote left after twenty minutes carrying a large chunk of cow remains. He went seventy yards along a sheep fence before turning up a woods road and into some pines. The place interested me because, although no crows had come to feed on the main cow remains on previous days, they had apparently been finding something back in the woods. The place the coyote had gone was where I had seen the crows dropping down among the pines. With the crows, as with ravens, coyotes seem to help determine how much carrion these birds get. Coyotes not only open up carcasses with tough hides so the birds can feed, they also drag pieces into the woods where crows and ravens prefer to feed. The second role is especially important when a carcass or gut pile is new, for, seemingly due to an instinctive wariness of new situations, the birds are usually afraid of it.

I have gotten much pleasure from my watchings at Walter Record's farm. Wildlife is not easy to see in winter months in New Hampshire, and before I started putting out food, the farm

woods and fields seemed desolate, cold, and deserted in months from November to March. But by keeping a feeding station going, I keep myself entertained.

TEN

WATCHING BY
A BEAVER POND

IN THE FIRST twenty years we lived in Lyme I explored widely
through woods and hills, looking mostly for places where I could
study woodpeckers and nuthatches. The best places were generally beaver ponds, either abandoned or still in use. They provided forest edges and an abundance of old stubs for roosting and
nesting. Beaver ponds were also good places for other kinds of
wildlife, and there were few around Lyme that I did not visit,
some many times. By far the best ponds, and the ones that I
visited daily in May, June, and July for a number of years, were
those in the Pickledish. I do not know where the name came
from, but the Pickledish was a series of ponds lying in a granite
basin. The woods of hemlock, spruce, and balsam that grew on
surrounding ledges, the abundance of lady's slippers, painted
trillium, and other flowers that bloomed in late spring, and the
near absence of people, at least in the morning hours when I did
my watching, made the Pickledish seem wild, isolated, and,
from my point of view, ideal.

In the course of my sitting on the banks of the main pond
watching the nestings of my woodpeckers, other birds and animals became used to me and, as often happens, my harvest of
observations was greater than I expected. I dressed warmly for
early-morning sessions but often got chilled when sitting for an
hour.

One morning at the Pickledish I stood up to stretch. I thought
what a day it was for a climb—just the day to ascend the cliff

above the pond. The climb was steep, but not long. When I reached the top, I found a small paradise. The stretches of gray, lichen-covered ledges, the low blueberry bushes, and the stunted spruces, looking out over hundreds of square miles of woods dotted by occasional lakes, made it seem like the summit of a mountain. How few signs of civilization! But it was the ponds below that attracted my attention most. The pond with a beaver lodge rising from its widest part was by far the largest. From my height I could see the white bellies of Tree Swallows flashing over the water, Common Grackles heading toward their nesting stubs, and a muskrat swimming toward the shore, propelled by its tail. Lying between the long dam of the main pond, and an even longer one of its own, lay a lagoon that stopped by the lumber road skirting it. Below the road and directly below the cliff, lay the lower pond. Here I could look down on kingbirds and a phoebe as a hawk might see them.

I walked the length of the lagoon every morning to cross its upper end and reach the place where I did my watching. I gradually became aware that although there was only one muskrat in the main pond and one in the lower pond, there were three in the smaller lagoon. The three got along well with one another, and I suspected that they had been born in the spring, probably in the central beaver lodge. Muskrats are common enough, but I had never lived in a place where I could watch them. Their usual habitat is among cattails that make watching difficult. But at the Pickledish, with its granite shores, there were no cattails, and there were few other obstructions to watching. I could count on seeing the muskrats nearly every morning.

The young muskrats became remarkably tame. When I stopped on my way in or out to look at a purple-fringed orchid or yellow loosestrife by the lagoon, I often noticed one or another of them floating motionless, eyeing me from a short distance. Sometimes one came even closer to feed. Had these muskrats, seeing me every day, decided I was harmless? On July 13 one of them crawled up among the jewelweed and other weeds growing on the dam, cut a stalk, then returned to the water to tow it to a semisubmerged landing. A second one crawled up beside it to feed on the same stalk. Other incidents indicated as well that the muskrats were friendly with each other. Two swam together, almost touching, then climbed a bank to feed side by side. Usually, however, they preferred to slip into the water to eat with bellies soaking as they held blades of bur-reed in their clenched fists. Their feeding generated small circular waves, which betrayed where they were even when the animals were hidden by clumps of vegetation. The fur of the muskrats was deep and soft and looked semidry even when they were swimming. This was in contrast to that of the beaver, which always looked sleek and wet, whether the animal was on land or in the pond.

The two single muskrats that occupied the main and lower ponds at the Pickledish lived in old beaver lodges. The three in the lagoon, with no old lodge to retire to, took shelter under a stump surrounded by water or in a hollow among the logs of the dam. The Pickledish, being a series of granite basins, offered no opportunities for burrowing.

How suitable a place was the Pickledish for muskrats, I wondered, considering that it had no cattails and no real marsh? In years past I hadn't seen muskrats there, and I think that a change in vegetation may have made life at the Pickledish more possible for the muskrats I observed there. Four years previously I had watched beaver feeding on a "grass" that grew in shallow water with blades turning at right angles when they reached the surface. There was but little of it then. Within a few years, however, it had become abundant and was a main food of the muskrat. To my surprise, as the water fell in June and July, the "grass" turned out to be bur-reed (*Sparganium*), a sturdy plant with white flowers and later seeds on which the muskrat fed.

What a quiet, beautiful spot the lagoon was! How happy the muskrats looked slipping into the water, or climbing out, like boys in a swimming hole. But supposing a mink, one of their main predators, should come along—what would happen then? When approaching the ponds on July 27, I saw a mink run from the lagoon, return, then dash across the lumber road to the lower pond. After running along several logs, it disappeared in a jumble of fallen trees. I could see a circle of telltale wavelets radiating out from the jumble. A muskrat was feeding in there. What was happening? Was the muskrat fleeing? No! To my surprise it was the mink that appeared. It bounded along logs close to the shore, then swam out, dove, and made for the outlet, as I could see by the train of bubbles it stirred from the bottom. And the muskrat? To my surprise, it paddled steadily after the mink, not making as good time, but in pursuit of it as far as the dam.

The mink was a large one, looking as large or even larger than the muskrat. Had the mink already fed on one of the lagoon juveniles and, being no longer hungry, paid no attention to the muskrat in the lower pond? I found later that the three juveniles were still in place as was the mother (as I called her) in the main pond. The five muskrats of the Pickledish were thus accounted for. Had the mink simply failed, then? Paul Errington, an expert on predation, says that mink prey mostly on surplus muskrats, those that are displaced, sick, or injured. With the Pickledish muskrats well established and healthy, the mink may have known that it stood little chance of killing one. It may have come to the ponds looking for other and smaller prey.

When I first came to the Pickledish another June the beaver were in a small upper pond where they had wintered. This uppermost pond has relatively little water at any time of year and none by the end of May. The beaver were thus forced down to their main pond. The first one I saw there was the mother beaver, "Bev" as I called her. Her behavior was much the same on several mornings. She swam to within ten to twelve feet of me to put mud on the dam, then floated and looked my way briefly before climbing over into the main pond. Once there she took a long swim to the central lodge. Most of her progress was underwater, bubbles marking her course. Every thirty feet or so she came to the surface to look around. Then, with a final dive, she disappeared in the lodge.

Bev decided to have a closer look at me on June 29 for, after reaching the lodge, she turned to patrol back and forth before the ledge where I sat. She made one *ker-splash* with her tail. Although I was to see her many times in July and early August, she never whacked the water again. I have always loved the splash of a beaver whacking the water. It is one of the grand sounds of nature. But as summer set in I was more excited to find that Bev and her mate did not seem to feel the need of splashing when I was around. I was by the pond every morning from early May until early August. While I did not see the beaver on most days, especially in the first two months, I imagined that they always saw or at least got wind of me and that from familiarity they came to accept me as part of the landscape.

Bev's mate took a longer time to accept me than did Bev. I had seen him only once before when, on July 22, I found the pair of them in the muskrat lagoon. Bev floated lazily about, then dove and came up within six feet of me. It was then that I noticed her mate at the end of the lagoon. He immediately headed for the main dam, and once in the water above, he gave a resounding splash. This was the only one he gave during the forty minutes that he was where I could watch him. When I reached my seat on the granite ledge, he swam over and patrolled back and forth, looking me over as Bev had done earlier in the month. Then he swam to join Bev by the central lodge. The two dove, went in, and came out several times. The water levels of the ponds were falling as a near-drought persisted, and of all the four old lodges in the ponds, the one they were moving into was in the deepest water.

It was not until August that I suspected the beaver might have young. When I arrived at my ledge on August 1, Bev was swimming away with a leafy ash spray in her teeth. She carried it to the lodge, dove, and went in. Her arrival set off a din of *un*s and *wun*s that went on for fifteen minutes. I had heard a few noises on previous mornings, but never anything like this. Bev was by the lodge again on the following morning. I now felt that I was making progress. While she swam slowly along as if looking for a place to climb out, I spotted her mate well up on a bank. How enormous he looked! A beaver looks much smaller in the water, when its haunches and hind feet are hidden, than on land when its whole bulk is exposed.

The male was gnawing bark from a hemlock root. After a few minutes he turned, facing me as he chewed a thick piece held in his paws. Bev suddenly climbed out of the water below and hauled herself up. The two beaver rested side by side, exchanging low *wun*s. This surprised me, for I had read that beaver only vocalize when in their lodge. After pausing, Bev moved on to gnaw at the hemlock root. She stood up twice to look up the trunk, but most of it that was within reach had been gnawed bare years before.

Bev finally turned and started back. She met her mate again, and the two put their heads together, nuzzling each other's fur. One raised its paw as if embracing. Both beaver then fell to browsing on the slope, which was bare except for moss and small plants—wild Canada mayflowers, checkerberry, low clintonias, and goldthread. Had sheep or goats been browsing, they would have made short work of what was there, but the beaver, with their powerful incisors adapted for gnawing down trees, made slow progress. When the sun finally flooded over the treetops, first the male, then Bev, slipped into the water to return to their lodge.

I continued to do well with the beaver for the next few days. Both swam about indifferent to my sitting in the open. They waddled ashore several times to feed among growths of various annuals, entering and leaving the bank by small canals that they had recently enlarged. With the beaver moving about as if I were not there and swimming at times within a dozen feet, I reflected, as with the muskrats, how welcome it was to feel for a time like one among other creatures. This may not seem like much to anyone unacquainted with beaver, but where they are trapped, or unfamiliar with intruders, they are likely to come out only at night and, if seen by day, to whack the water in alarm before disappearing.

A feature of the Pickledish was that the beaver and muskrat

seemed to work in shifts, the beaver staying out until the sun first appeared over the trees, then retiring as the muskrats began to become active. This was most striking at the central lodge, where the "mother" muskrat swam out at 7:00 A.M. one day as the last of the two beaver entered for the day. The lodge was so large and old that I imagined the muskrat had a hole and chamber for itself separate from the beaver.

The temperaments of the two animals were very different. Whereas the beaver seemed to enjoy floating or swimming about in a leisurely way, the muskrats, propelled by rapid motions of their tails, were always busy as they went about gathering food. I felt that "busy as a muskrat" was more apt an expression than "busy as a beaver." The American Indians made the same observation long ago. I have long been interested in Indians, and one of my treasured books is Charles Eastman's *Indian Boyhood*. Eastman was a Sioux, one of only a few Indians who went through Dartmouth College in the nineteenth century. He was brought up by his grandmother who, he wrote, "worked like a beaver in those days (or rather like a muskrat, as the Indians say; for this industrious little animal sometimes collects as many as six or eight bushels of edible roots for the winter, only to be robbed of his store by some of our people)."

I had seen muskrat, beaver, and a mink at the Pickledish, and later I was to see a family of otters, but there remained another North American aquatic mammal that I had not encountered. I longed to see one, although I never expected to have the luck. Then one morning, when I was sitting particularly still as Bev swam close, the unbelievable happened. A water shrew, with prey of some kind in its jaws, suddenly popped from the water onto a semisubmerged log at my feet, ran along with nose and whiskers in the air, then disappeared. It was only a glimpse, but it was, for me, a high point of my watching.

In another year, 1981, I saw nothing of beaver in the first days of June when I came to the Pickledish ponds to watch the nesting of a pair of Downy Woodpeckers. The nest was in a stub standing in open water, so that I had a good chance to look out over the main pond. It was on my third morning that a beaver swam below the Downy's nest. What she was doing I could not tell. She swam up and down past a small rocky island, often submerging, and on one occasion towing a sodden branch. I called her "Bev" with no way of knowing whether she was the same "Bev" I had watched in a previous year.

I saw nothing of Bev in the following week of cloudy weather. By the time the Downies had fledged and the sun had returned, I had moved to the opposite shore to watch a flicker's nest. The islet where I had seen Bev lay halfway between the two nests. I had hardly settled to watch the flickers when Bev came swimming toward the islet towing the trunk of a small tree ten feet long. I now had a better view, and it was a thrill to see Bev climb onto her lodge with the log in her teeth, then push it among the mess of logs and branches already there. She seemed to have no plan, but her aimlessness was deceptive. I slowly recognized that the messy conglomeration of sticks was taking on a shape. Bev was building a lodge! Her massive haunches, supported by her large feet and broad tail, were marvelously adapted to pulling and pushing. She was in no hurry. I particularly enjoyed the leisurely way she floated about in the water. The pond was her domain, and she seemed to take pleasure in surveying it. She rarely returned to her work without taking a dive to dredge a snag from the bottom to carry back. Hearing a splashing one morning, I moved over to find Bev hauling and yanking at a snag caught in a tangle. Once she had it free she paddled through a channel to deposit it on the lodge. She then came to a ledge only sixteen feet from me to feed on grass and sedges. What a satisfaction to find her paying so little attention to me! It was nearly eleven before Bev returned to her lodge for good, the longest that I had ever seen her out.

I had seen a second, somewhat smaller beaver on several occasions—the male, I presumed. He had never swum close to the new lodge, at least he hadn't with his head above water. I knew that females are the dominant partners around a beaver pond, especially when about to have young. Perhaps this was why her mate kept away.

I did not visit the pond for several days after July 1. When I returned I found Bev had been adding mud and sticks to her lodge and that it now rose three feet above the water. She climbed to the top of it at about 7:00 A.M. to drag up a few more sticks, then disappeared. At close to 8:00 I became aware that things were going on inside. I had heard no vocalizations in June. Now I suddenly heard great numbers of them, similar to the ones I had heard coming from the main lodge in the previous summer. The vocalizations were almost continuous. I circled the shore to listen. The nearest I could get was twenty feet. The mixture of sounds came in waves lasting a minute or two; then after a pause of thirty seconds they began again. If my guess was correct, Bev must have had a litter at about the time she completed the lodge. I listened to the sounds for nearly an hour. All I heard on succeeding mornings were occasional *wun*s. I continued to watch, but I saw no more of Bev and noted that she was no longer adding sticks. Her maternity lodge seemed to have been finished in the nick of time.

On looking into a number of books about beaver, I was astonished that none of the authors seemed to have actually watched them building lodges. Most lodges are built or rebuilt in the fall, usually after dark. I was probably lucky in being able to watch Bev building her small lodge on sunny mornings. Prospective mothers, I gathered from reading, do not build special lodges in most years, and I just happened upon the right year to see Bev building one. Possibly the other lodges at the Pickledish were too old and crumbling or were not surrounded by enough water to be safe for housing a new litter.

I was disappointed in the first books I read about beaver, knowing what affectionate and social creatures they are from one that Jane, I, and the children had raised. It was given to us by a game warden who had found it, probably not a week old, floating on the water after he had blown up a dam. We kept this original "Bev" in a large aquarium in the center of our kitchen for a year, taking it out periodically to give it the run of the house. One of Bev's occupations at these times was to dam the doorways of the kitchen with sticks of firewood and other objects, then tip over the dog's water dish by way of making a pond. Bev liked to be picked up and petted and never tried to bite any of us or to gnaw the furniture.

I eventually found two books on the beaver written with understanding: one by Lars Wilsson, *My Beaver Colony*, and the other, *Beaversprite* by Dorothy Richards. Mrs. Richards' book appeals to me particularly because she not only raised beaver by hand but also, with great patience, tamed wild ones to the extent of having them come into her house in the Adirondacks and sit around her armchair. She followed her wild and tame beavers for over twenty years and learned much about them. While my observations of the beaver are obviously fragmentary, I would never have been able to appreciate the work of Wilsson and Richards had I not made them.

I paid few visits to the Pickledish ponds in the latter part of the summer. Rains increased in September, reaching a crescendo in the last few days of the month. Red and yellow leaves, beaten down and sodden by rain, were already beginning to carpet the ground when I climbed to the Pickledish on October 1. After the summer drought it was pleasant to find the ponds full and water gurgling through the dams. The beaver had left the small lodge built in June for the large one in the center of the pond, as I could see from bright, freshly gnawed logs lying on top of it. The ponds, however, seemed lifeless without the Tree Swallows and other summer birds. But what was that splashing? Could it be ducks? I edged closer for a look—and what a thrill! The splashing was from a family of otters.

On first view the otters looked like a school of porpoises as they rolled forward to dive, with backs and rear ends humping up. Here and there a tail followed a roll or even waved in the air. The swimming and diving made steady sounds of moving, lightly disturbed water. At times three heads came up, moved abreast, then rolled under. What was going on? There have never been any fish in the Pickledish, so I concluded that the otters must be either after crayfish or more likely frogs, especially green frogs and their large tadpoles. The frogs and tadpoles might, expectedly, have concentrated in the deeper parts of the pond with the onset of cold weather.

The otters turned after a bit and worked their way back to climb on a floating log, shake themselves, run a short way, then slip into the water again. Their graceful, sinuous motions seemed like play. They moved so rapidly that I found them difficult to count. I was sure at first that there were three, but it took time to see that there was a fourth, too, which sometimes followed its own course. I suspected that, being a little larger, it was an adult and the others were juveniles. The otters now came close. I felt as if I were in the front row of a zoo as they climbed on logs and stumps and rollicked about fifteen to twenty feet away. They next headed for the large beaver lodge in the center of the pond. The juveniles scrambled to the top, bobbing their heads as they looked down at the larger otter below. Was the parent, if such it was, communicating with them? The wind had veered. Possibly the otters had my scent. In any event they took to the water again and headed for the maternity lodge built in June. One ran over the top, then dove and came up inside where, for some seconds, I heard pleasant growly sounds as the family gathered inside. Then silence.

It had not occurred to me that otters would come to the Pickledish, which was devoid of fish, yet here was a family of them having a grand time and apparently much at home. Had they driven the beaver and their young from their summer lodge, or worse, had they killed and eaten the young, forcing the parents to move back to the old lodge? Leonard Lee Rue III, in his book *The World of the Beaver*, gives a photo of an otter, labeled as "the beaver's greatest natural enemy." But is this so? There seems to be no evidence that otter, with their relatively small teeth suited to catching fish, prey on anything as large and

formidable as beaver. Only wolves are known to do so regularly. It would seem, on the contrary, from Hope Buyukmichi's book *Hour of the Beaver* that families of the two species can swim around together in perfect amity.

As I have remarked earlier, one of the greatest assets in behavior watching is to be with birds or animals that are relatively tame. You may find them tame, or by going to a place every day as I did at the Pickledish, you may get animals used to seeing you around. Hugh Miles, in his book *The Track of the Wild Otter*, describes a similar approach, which he used in the Shetland Islands. After walking about for some time and seeing little, he wrote:

> Walking these shores day after day I have become immersed in the scene. Gulls no longer jump up in alarm, curlews merely look up and continue to feed, rabbits just watch me pass by. It gives me a feeling of warmth to be accepted by these wild creatures and I settle into my hiding place to enjoy this new-found freedom. I imagine the otter must be very sensitive to this atmosphere of peace and I am pleased that I too am learning to feel the pulse of the shore, becoming a natural part of this beautiful wilderness.

Another aspect of tameness is that wild animals living in extremely remote places may have no fear of man. Two recent accounts especially arouse my envy and admiration: one concerning a family of arctic wolves that David Mech watched on Ellesmere Island, and the other, Mark and Delia Owens' account of the desert lions that lay about their camp in the Kalahari in southern Africa. Not having seen man before, the lions accepted the Owenses with an astonishing lack of concern. The experiences of these authors give us a glimpse of the kind of relations our hunter ancestors may have had with other creatures in the millions of years over which our brain evolved. How I wish I could spend even an hour in Ellesmere with Mech's wolves or with the Owenses' lions in the Kalahari! But then how wonderful, I think, that with a little imagination, the patience to sit, and a love of animals, I can have much the same kind of experience without traveling far from where I live. "Can a youth, a man," wrote Thoreau, " do more wisely than to go where his life is to be found?"

ELEVEN

BIRDS AT THE PICKLEDISH

ABRAHAM LINCOLN, when asked how long he went to school, said one year, and not all at once but only "by littles." In the same manner I have been building up life histories of common birds, not all at once, but in snatches when I have had the opportunity, for I find everything about birds interesting. Studying birds in one's own yard sounds ideal, but is not always easy. Birds have a way of disappearing around corners of houses, across the street, or up in tall trees where it is hard to catch a glimpse of them. I was pleased, therefore, to find that I was able to catch up on some birds by the beaver ponds of the Pickledish that I had not been able to follow very well at home.

Bev came over the main dam into the muskrats' lagoon in early June and swam to within twelve feet of where I stood. *Ker-splash.* She whacked with her tail, and a spray of water sparkled in the morning sun. A male kingbird flew into the spray like a flash and did so again when Bev, emerging from a dive, sent up another spray.

The activities of the kingbird's mate were less spectacular. When I came to the lower pond a few days later, I found her struggling where a pole had lodged against a dead hemlock. The hemlock stood in water fifteen feet from the shore. What was she trying to do? Perhaps I had better watch. After a few minutes she flew to an abandoned beaver lodge, scanned it for some moments, then returned with a twig in her bill. Like Bev building

148

her small maternity lodge, she was building a nest in the open and without the aid of her mate.

It took the female kingbird four days to build her nest. She did the shaping by lifting her body and shuffling with her feet while using her bill to pull ends in place. The nest was ideal for watching. It was completely in the open and the kingbird pair, being bold by nature, did not mind my standing on the bank nearby. What handsome birds kingbirds are when seen close with a pair of field glasses!

Regardless of what else I might be watching at the Pickledish in June and July, it was difficult to go more than a few minutes without catching a glimpse of the male kingbird. He was forever patrolling the pond and attacking other birds, from Common Grackles, Tree Swallows, and flickers, to sapsuckers and goldfinches. Hearing odd noises coming from the sky one morning, I looked up to see a raven flying high above with the male kingbird almost riding on its back. A raven might rob a kingbird's nest, and so there was some sense to the male's attacking one. But why was the kingbird's aggressiveness triggered so often by lesser targets? After it had returned to perch over my head, it paid no attention to a flicker resting close by. But when a goldfinch flew past at some distance, the kingbird attacked at once, the two birds turning and twisting as the smaller bird sought to escape.

Why should the kingbird have attacked a goldfinch well away from its nest? I think the belligerence of kingbirds is, in part, the way males keep themselves in trim. The only way they can get away with nesting completely in the open is to be forever on the alert. Attacking goldfinches or other harmless neighbors keeps a male on the go and ready for any hawk, raven, or other real threat that may come along. What doubtless counts in attacks against large birds is speed and surprise. Male kingbirds become proficient in these tactics by practicing on smaller neighbors.

I had planned to follow the nesting of the kingbirds in the lower pond, but after the eggs had been laid and incubated a week, their nest, the one balanced precariously on a leaning pole, fell into the water.

It was three years before I found another kingbird nest convenient for watching. But it again took a few days to find out what
the kingbirds were doing as they built the nest. With quivering
flights, white underparts gleaming and tails outspread to show
the white terminal bands, one or the other of the pair were always
in the open. Where were they going to nest? The female snuggled down on various stubs arising from the pond, but none
seemed suitable. On the third day, I was excited to find her
bringing sticks to the base of a branch twenty feet above the
water. She worked hard collecting twigs from a dead hemlock
and sometimes from the top of a beaver lodge, her mate flying
along as a fighter escort wherever she went.

Her greatest difficulties were in getting the sticks to stay in
place. They dangled in spite of her efforts and, on this first
morning, it seemed that for each one added, another fell into the
water. I left after a few hours thinking the situation hopeless.
The female was more resourceful than I supposed, however. By
the following morning she was flying to a black cherry, pulling
billfuls of silk from tent caterpillar nests, then flying back to
wipe silk over the unmanageable sticks. Thanks to the silk, the
sticks now held together, and she was soon shaping a nest by
pushing with her breast and kicking with her feet.

An initial difficulty in watching kingbirds was telling the
sexes apart. I was gratified, therefore, on discovering early that
the male and female had separate duties. While she built the
nest, incubated the eggs, and brooded the young, he stayed at a
distance on guard until the eggs hatched and the nestlings were
ready to be fed. When she flew off the nest while incubating, he
stayed near it, flying out to hover before her by way of greeting
her on her return.

The most enjoyable hours I spent with the kingbirds at the
Pickledish were during their last week of nesting. While half of
the items brought to the nestlings were too small to identify, the
other half consisted of dragonflies. How could small nestlings be
expected to swallow such large, ungainly insects? I soon found
that both parents were experts. It took only one deft poke to send

the four wings, long abdomen, and six legs of a dragonfly down the gullet of a clamoring youngster.

One of the things that attracted me to the kingbirds was their alertness while foraging. Their heads were constantly turning this way and that, like a hawk's, when the kingbirds were on the lookout for a dragonfly. Once one was sighted, the kingbird swooped. Not all forays were successful: I noted many a fast pursuit in which the dragonfly escaped. A kingbird hit the water on rare occasions, coming up with a small frog which it beat against a branch before flying with it to the nest.

In 1980 I saw the male kingbird make many attacks on a pair of Blue Jays that nested at the edge of adjacent woods, and once he mounted high to attack a hawk. What I could not understand was why he attacked Tree Swallows with special severity. Four of fourteen attacks made on swallows near the nest were mild enough, even when a swallow perched only six feet from the nestlings. The severe attacks were all on swallows flying close to the water, well away from the nest. The attacks were made so quickly that it was hard to see the details, but it looked as though the kingbird was trying to force the swallows into the water. What impressed me was the similarity of the attacks to those made on dragonflies. Could the male kingbird, catching sight of a swallow skimming the surface, have regarded it as a superdragonfly, something worth trying to catch?

I was surprised at how much the female brooded her young in the last days of nesting. In addition to brooding in the cool of early morning, she spent considerable time protecting her young from the sun at midday and even brooded the last nestling for five minutes, a mere twenty-five minutes before it left the nest.

I had wondered earlier whether I would have the luck to be on hand at the moment of the kingbird's nest-leaving. When the mother came to feed the last of her two nestlings for the final time, she came close, then moved away eight inches as if trying to entice it to leave. It followed her at once, begging lustily.

I found the parents flying repeatedly to one place in a leafy tree on the following morning. Did this mean that only one fledgling had survived? I did not learn until the next day that the two fledglings stuck closely together. If one flew to a new tree, the other followed, moving along branches until it could snuggle against its sibling as if the two were still in the nest. After a parent had fed a young one it rested near it for a minute or two. When both parents rested close the kingbirds made a family group of four. They kept to an area of shore within seventy feet of the old nest for the first week after fledging. I had thought the male would now be free of his nest-time aggressiveness. On July 5, however, three days after the young had left the nest, he made a severe attack on a robin, grappling with it in midair.

The family of kingbirds remained by the pond for ten days before disappearing. They may have returned to the pond to roost, for I found the four of them together in the nest tree on two successive early mornings. It seemed that, even though away by day, they returned to roost by the pond at night.

When the young finally left the Pickledish the parents returned as a pair. Their behavior was now different. The male hovered above his mate and accompanied her closely as in the early breeding season. On July 20, eighteen days after their young had fledged, the pair were by the old nest tree. The female snuggled down into crotches of several bare stubs, as if prospecting for a second nest site, and the male attacked a Hairy Woodpecker. The kingbirds were, I believed, having a revival of courtship. But the revival lasted only a few days. The last I saw of the kingbirds was on August 2. The two were on the same perch. Moving along the granite ledge for a better look, I saw that the male had caught a dragonfly of the largest size and was having difficulties subduing it. His mate hovered close as if excited. After slinging the prize sideways, the male tossed it into the air, recaught the dragonfly, and swallowed it. The female now captured a dragonfly, and like her mate, had difficulty subduing it. This time the captor was surrounded by three chickadees and a Yellow-rumped Warbler, attracted, it seemed, by the spectacle of a kingbird struggling with so large an item of prey. The kingbirds now perched three feet apart to rest and preen. I hoped that, bringing with them memories of good dragonfly hunting, the two would return another year.

The most conspicuous birds at the beaver ponds in May and June, the kingbirds, grackles, and Tree Swallows, were all species that also nested or came to our yard. There the grackles were almost impossible to watch no matter how far away I remained. None would come to their nests at the top of tall white pines while I was watching. Robins let me do all the watching I wanted to, but not the grackles. This frustrated me for some years, for I have long considered grackles as one of the more beautiful as well as the more intelligent of common birds. What surprised me at the Pickledish was finding that grackles can nest in two very different situations: near the top of tall white pines, balsams, and other conifers; and in decayed stubs in beaver ponds.

A female grackle at the Pickledish paused on May 30 with long dead grass stalks in her bill at the water edge of the main beaver lodge, as if waiting for me to move on. I looked away, and I believe that within seconds, seeing that I did not have my eye on her, she flew to her nest and deposited the grass. After a few minutes she was at the top of the lodge waiting with another billful. This time I watched her for ten minutes. Again it was when I looked away that she went to the nest in a flash and was off without the grass. That sharp eye of hers, with its yellow iris, must have been regarding me intently. By the third time she came to the beaver lodge in a half-hour, I think she was becoming more used to me for, with me continuing to sit still, she settled without waiting in the crotch of a yellow birch stub two feet above the water. I saw her nest at last!

Having found one grackle's nest I moved to a granite ledge where I could watch another female. I soon noticed that she, unlike the beaver-lodge female, made an almost incessant *chack*ing. It was only when I moved away and watched from a distance that she entered a crotch in a decayed yellow birch and her *chack*ing stopped. I was surprised at what a small cavity she had squeezed herself into. The cleft left her no room to turn around.

Having found two nests, I decided that here was an opportunity to watch grackles at last and that I had better make the most of it. When I returned in a few days I noticed some changes at the beaver-lodge nest. When the female grackle left to feed, her mate came to a perch about forty feet away and remained there guarding until she returned. When she returned I was gratified to have her come direct to the nest rim without paying any attention to me. Her inattention may have been in part because a pair of Tree Swallows, nesting in a hole only three feet above, were swooping on her.

Her mate, meanwhile, was walking along a stretch of shore against a background of small sedges, Canada mayflower, and bunchberry. With his sharp yellow eye, and his bronze-and-purple iridescence showing in the sun, especially when he spread his tail and held his wings a little out in giving his *zaire* note, the male grackle was a handsome sight. He caught something, possibly a tadpole, that took some pecking to consume. At last I was learning a little bit about the life of the grackle. My bird walked mostly along sunken logs and, at the end of one of them, stopped to take a vigorous bath. He then flew to a high perch to preen, but when a Blue Jay flew across the pond, he flew to attack it.

I noticed on succeeding days that the behavior of the two female grackles was markedly different. The female of the yellow birch was the noisiest bird around the Pickledish. Scared to approach her nest, even when I was some distance away, she made loud *chack*s at rates of 180 a minute, interspersed with *jer, jer*s that sounded like an electric buzzer. Sometimes, with food in her bill, she would spend from ten to thirteen minutes *chack*ing before taking it to her young. Although the yellow birch female was more advanced in her nesting, I do not think having older young made all the difference between her and the female by the beaver lodge, who was quiet and relatively tame. On June 12 the latter preened herself on the beaver lodge for a few minutes, walked out on a stick nearest to her nest, making a few *chack*s, took a drink, and then, in no hurry, slipped onto her eggs. Once she was settled, all that I could see was her bill, the top of her head, and her bright yellow eye, her feathers and bill making a small patch of jet black against the weathered gray wood of the nest stub. Her young hatched the next day.

It was at this time that I saw a curious behavior when the female grackle left her nest. Circling low over the water, she landed on a log in a marshy place and, with head and tail up, immediately pushed her breast down against the log, her wings held out and quivering in the position of a female soliciting copulation. Why she should have acted thus at the time her eggs hatched, I do not know. Possibly it was general excitement arising from the hatching of her young. Two males in trees above paid no apparent attention to her.

Much of the nesting by the Pickledish was ending by July. Tree Swallows and grackles, the most conspicuous of the birds, left early in the month, and I anticipated that I would soon have little to look at. Quite unexpected, therefore, was a second wave of nestings that went on into August. A pair of Red-breasted Nuthatches fledged a first brood in early June and were nesting again by the end of the month. Their second nest was in a stub standing in open water, and the pair did not mind my sitting within a dozen feet of the entrance to watch their comings and goings. It was a continuing delight to hear the male burst into a melodious shower of notes when he passed an insect to his mate through the opening in the stub. She joined in the singing and continued to sing by herself nearly a minute after he had left. I know of no birds that display more domestic felicity than Red-breasted Nuthatches.

A family of Northern Yellowthroats, the parents and their fledged young, were active in bushes not far from the nut-hatches. They were not at all shy, the male coming out on July 16 to sing and preen in the sun near where I sat. The two juveniles were moving about in a thicket below. When one flew up with wings quivering and bill open begging for food, the

male paid no attention. I supposed that, with the juveniles able
to forage for themselves, he was now free from parental cares.
How wrong I was! A short way beyond the granite ledge where I
did much of my watching, beaver had made several shallow
basins to catch water from the runoff of melting snow in the
spring. By July these basins were nothing but stretches of dark
earth. It was in a tangle of vegetation by one of these, I discovered, that the yellowthroats had built a second nest. On July 19,
three days after the day I had concluded that the male was
through for the season, I found him stuffing his bill with insects
as he had done for nestlings in June. All I had to do to make him
appear was to sit down on a stump in one of the dry basins. I had
hardly sat down on July 22 when he came to a stump twelve feet
away. Shafts of sunlight, coming through the trees, lighted up
his yellow thoat and black mask as he turned this way and that,
all the while making slight jerky motions with his tail. What a
beautiful bird! One yellowthroat well seen in its natural surroundings, is enough to make a morning.

The male had his bill crammed with the largest wad of soft-
bodied insects that I had ever seen him carry. Gauzy wings and
long abdomens hung down on either side like a droopy mous-
tache. The bird could not have made himself more conspicuous.
Then the male suddenly cocked his tail and began shivering his
wings violently. His mate had arrived. She also had prey in her
bill and was, like him, afraid to go to the nest. One of the
juveniles, with wings quivering, kept pressing close to one
parent or the other to get the food, but neither parent paid any
attention. The time for feeding juveniles was over. When I
moved farther back, the parents went into the thicket and came
back with their bills empty, more or less spotting for me where
their second nest was located.

When I sat on my stump on the next two mornings, it was
mainly the female that came out into the open, moving across
the bare earth in long hops only ten feet from me. At the end of a
half-circle, she came even closer, shivering her wings and pressing her head and breast low. Her distraction displays interested

me especially because in usual Northern Yellowthroat habitat marshy vegetation would have prevented me from seeing them at all well. Thanks to the basins provided by the beaver I could not have seen the displays to better advantage. I did not go to her nest, knowing that if I trampled the vegetation, a raccoon or other predator would be almost sure to find it.

Cedar Waxwings were another bird whose nestings I had not studied much previously. I found a pair at the Pickledish on July 4. The waxwings were carrying stems of samaras from a maple to a place forty feet up in a leafy tree. I craned my neck, looking up from varying angles, but the situation was hopeless. All I got was a stiff neck from trying to see what the birds were doing. As a nest to watch in the way I like to watch a nest, this one was too high. But when I sat down to rest I noted a second pair of waxwings. One flew to a kingbird's nest, now vacated, and pulled out a twig. Waxwings often use the deserted nests of other birds in this way. It was a simple matter for me to follow the waxwing with the twig to the spreading branch of a hemlock. Here was a perfect nest for watching: low down and without obstructing vegetation. On the following morning I brought my folding chair and sat at my ease while watching developments.

In the few articles that I could find on the nesting of waxwings, which like to nest in small colonies, the authors said they could find no signs of territoriality. But on July 5 I saw signs of it when the pair of the hemlock branch came to feed among grasses not far from the nest tree of the first pair. The latter flew down to displace the intruders. The conflicts were mild. One reason I happened to see them, I believe, was that territorial behavior among many kinds of birds reaches a peak at the time of nest-building, falling away thereafter. I had come upon the waxwings at just the right time.

Another behavior I did not find described by others until later was the way the male waxwing feeds his mate during incubation. It is common enough in the non-nesting season to see one waxwing pass a berry to another, but what I saw by the pond was no such casual affair. When the male returned from foraging with his throat full of food but none in his bill, the female flew to him. Many female birds shiver their wings in begging. Not the female waxwing. She held her wings out sideways and rotated them in somewhat the manner of wooden ducks set up on poles in the wind. As the female pushed up against her mate, he pumped food into her open bill four or five times, then moved away. She did not want him to get off so easily. She kept right after him, paddling her wings as furiously as ever, in spite of his having nothing more to give. Perhaps this was her way of letting him know how urgent her need was. After he had left, the female waxwing returned to her nest, undisturbed by my sitting fifteen feet away.

Many male birds feed their incubating mates on the nest. Why, I thought, didn't the male waxwing? He tried to at the start of incubation, but only once. His mate was sitting quietly as he approached, but she rose up and paddled vigorously when he arrived, making the nest conspicuous as she did so. Better, it would seem from a survival point of view, for her to slip off quietly and meet her mate at a distance where her paddling would do no harm.

Another engrossing bird at the Pickledish was the kingfisher. Jane and I once raised three nestling kingfishers, ones brought to us when their nest tunnel, in a gravel pit, fell open. The orphans did well in a nest I built for them in a box in my library, and when they were fledged and ready to fly I liberated them in the yard. They stayed around for a few days, diving into a plastic pool for goldfish, then left to forage on their own. I thus missed the opportunity of watching the further development of what I had come to feel were very interesting birds. I was therefore excited when three juvenile kingfishers came to the Pickledish for a week in midsummer. Their coming seemed almost providential in enabling me to pick up the life of the kingfisher where I had left off with my hand-raised trio.

My first view of one of the Pickledish kingfishers was on July 28, when I caught sight of a male downing a large tadpole. He caught two more in the next ten minutes. When the bird slung the last one sideways in preparation for swallowing, as kingfishers do with fish, the large head and the body of the tadpole broke off and fell into the water. A tadpole, the kingfisher may have learned, is not put together as solidly as a fish. The male swallowed the tail and left. When a female juvenile chased him five times, in, out, and around the trees and stubs of the pond, the white of the birds' underparts and their relatively large wings and bills made them a spectacular sight.

The kingfishers were wary, and I had to sit very still as I watched them. On August 1, I watched one of the two females for nearly two hours. She was hard to see when all that was exposed were her blue back and large, blackish head as seen from the rear. The colors did not stand out against the woods. When she faced me the case was different. The white on her breast, with two large bands across it, the lower one russet, made her conspicuous. Kingfishers make curious, spasmodic movements on alighting. The head, neck, and breast jerk, then the stubby tail, all upward. Why these movements? I can only guess that, as the colors of a kingfisher do not always stand out from afar, the distinctive jerkings are enough to proclaim, "I am a kingfisher. This is my territory." Kingfishers are, from my observations, territorial along streams and watercourses the year around. The head and tail movements made on alighting could be a way of spacing individuals out with a minimum of conflicts.

The female kingfisher I was watching usually perched not far above the water. On a first dive she came up with a small frog. She tried to beat it sideways, but it got away. Sometime later she made a second catch. I could not identify the prey for sure, but it looked like a newt. I wish I could have seen it more clearly. Our hand-raised kingfishers refused newts, which are known to have poison in their skins. The female at the pond downed her prey, whatever it was, and soon after caught another frog. This one also got away, but she was perched close to the water and retrieved it. My last view of her was on the lower pond. There she plunged completely under to catch a tadpole. A few slings, however, and it escaped. Thus of four catches, three got away with one retrieved. These signs of inexperience, as I took them to be, made me think that the kingfishers were all juveniles.

The juvenile kingfishers were particularly lively on the warm, sunny day of August 4. One of the females splashed the water four times in succession as she flew low over the pond, as if taking a bath, then alighted on a snag to preen. After diving and catching a frog, she splashed the water three more times. Not long afterward she was attacked by the second female. On being attacked the first one held her fully spread wings out sideways in a threat display. This was the last I saw of the kingfishers at the Pickledish. They meant a lot to me, for I had tried for some years in various places to sit down and watch kingfishers, with almost no success. They were always too quick in taking alarm. My observations at the Pickledish were not extensive, but they gave me a feeling that I had gotten a start with kingfishers.

No place could have been more favorable for pond-watching than the Pickledish, with its beaver and muskrat, its kingbirds and grackles, and its butterflies and flowers. With so much to watch I never tried to study any one thing until I found a favorable opportunity of doing so. There was one form of life on the ponds, however, that invited watching every time I visited the place. These were the whirligig beetles, which swarmed on the ponds' surface in enormous numbers. The beetles were not as noticeable when spread about widely in the sun at midday as they were in the cool of early mornings when they gathered in rafts, some-times a yard or two in extent. At one moment they looked like a solid mass of little black-domed bodies. Then—presto!—there would be an explosion as beetles in one part of a raft suddenly went berserk, tearing off at top speed in all directions without regard to how many other beetles were in the way. This set the whole mass a-rushing, with the result that the whirligigs were, within seconds, in an expanded area of roiled water. One might think from a distance that some underwater spring had suddenly erupted. But within less than a minute the beetles reassembled. To rest? Not for long. In minutes they would explode again. The repeated explosions in numbers of places over the mirrorlike suface of the pond, were a striking phenomenon for which I have been unable to find an explanation. Are they due to the release of some pheromone, or chemical messenger that passes from one insect to another, and if so, what role do they play in the life of the beetles?

I supposed that the quarter-inch whirligig beetles lived on prey too small for me to see. Then one bright afternoon I found twelve to twenty of them moving about in a tusseling mass. It took only a few moments to see that there was an object moving about below them. When the object rolled, I recognized it as a dead green-frog tadpole. A hundred other whirligigs hovered within a radius of a yard or so, one or another of them darting in to win a place in the struggle as some other one left. The tadpole, rolling about under their attacks, suggested a small whale being flensed.

With so many things to watch at the Pickledish, I came to feel frustrated that I was not learning much about the frogs and other amphibians which were so much a part of life of the ponds. Then on June 17 of one year, which I thought too late a date, I heard toads trilling. Where were they? From one side of the pond they sounded to be on the other and vice versa when I walked around. On the next morning, seated on my granite ledge, I did better. It was a cool, clear morning, and I felt that just to sit there and enjoy the reflections of sky and trees in the still, dark water was enough. Then, presumably because I was no longer moving, the toads began. Their trilling was a symphony played against the background of the forest pond, rising and falling as toads from far or near around the shore joined in or dropped away. Then, after some minutes, the trilling died down altogether, not to be resumed for a half-hour.

On the next go-around a disturbance in the water attracted my attention. Several toads were clambering onto a half-submerged log. Then I spotted two more already there. The four rested, paying no attention to one another. Only one, its throat ballooned out like a piece of bubble gum, joined the trilling that was going on around the pond. Another toad, even closer to me, climbed onto a log of his own and, at the closest range of my field glasses, sat with arms bent facing me, the gold of his pop eyes gleaming in the sun. When his throat ballooned into a trill, it was as if he were giving me a special performance.

Two days, and the trilling was over. I heard none later. The toads made me think of what an incredible reservoir of beauty there is in nature and how much of it is all too easily missed. "In health," wrote Thoreau, "the sound of a cow bell is celestial music." Is this not true of many other sounds if one is rested and receptive? I even came, in my months at the Pickledish, to take joy in the hum of mosquitoes. It also, if listened to, can help to make one's pulse beat with nature.

With little rain, the mud flats around the edges of the Pickledish ponds grew more extensive as summer progressed. When birds became fewer after the begining of August, I was ready to stay away until, as I hoped would happen, autumn rains raised the water levels. In the first week in August 1983, however, I had several experiences that I would not have missed. Jewelweed grew luxuriantly on the beaver dams and in a few places along the shore. One of these was on a rotting log below where I sat on my granite ledge. Once I got my feet down, the plants closed in around my knees. When I sat still it was not long before a hummingbird visited the trumpet-shaped flowers of the jewel-weed, first by a weathered stump, then by my knees. The tiny bird was almost in my hands. What a thrill to have it so close! I could look down on the burnished bronze of its back and the black-and-white markings of its spread tail.

The hummer was one of many thrills that came to me from sitting still and, as it were, merging with nature. One morning while watching on my ledge I had an extra dividend. The hummer was collecting nectar from jewelweeds when I noticed a pickerel frog that had climbed two feet up a stump to look out over the pond. When I saw these two exquisite creatures within a few inches of each other, it was almost painful to think how little I knew about either of them. When one feels ignorant of something relating to conventional knowledge, he can go to a library and look up the information, but this doesn't always work for things in nature. Only so much as one has discovered with one's own eyes has meaning. Taking things secondhand can never be a substitute. And what a place for this kind of natural history the Pickledish was! I thought of coming back another spring and summer to concentrate on the frogs and other aquatic life, but this was not to be.

By the time I was ready to return, bulldozers had moved in, and the Pickledish was no more.

There is probably no greater barrier for most people to watching birds or animals, or to studying anything else, for that matter, than the idea of being alone. From going on a number of Audubon trips in several states I have concluded that their group character is one of their greatest attractions. Yet throughout the ages thoughtful and creative people have cherished times of solitutude. "Ah wretched, and too solitary he, / Who loves not his own company," wrote Abraham Cowley in the seventeenth century and, in our own, Anne Morrow Lindbergh, whose book *Gift of the Sea* is one that I have on a shelf with Thoreau, wrote, "Certain springs are tapped only when we are alone." This is not the feeling of our times, however, for, as Mrs. Lindbergh continues, "As far as the search for solitude is concerned, we live in a negative atmosphere as invisible, as all pervasive and as enervating as high humidity on an August afternoon. The world does not understand the need to be alone."

When I sat alone for hundreds of hours by the Pickledish, I was never alone. If you love nature, you know how companionable it is. The hummingbird that came close to me, the pickerel frog, the whirligig beetles, the beaver that I got to know, all were part of me. Most birders cannot understand this truth. Go to some "hot spot," go where others go, seems to be their credo. So many did this at Holt's Ledge, not far from the Pickledish, that a pair of Peregrines seeking to nest there were too disturbed to do so.

TWELVE

INSTINCT FOR BEAUTY
AND
LOVE OF ANIMALS

WHEN I SPOKE to a scientific colleague about a sense of beauty, he said there is no such thing. Some people think a factory chimney beautiful, and others think it is the opposite. For my part I think a sense of the beauty of nature is innate. It was probably implanted in our ancestors early on. The sense of beauty had homeostatic value for man living in a state of nature: it made him feel at home in the world and in balance with other living things. "I thought the sparrow's note from heaven, singing at dawn on the alder bough," wrote Emerson. Who knows but that our remote hunter ancestors had the same awareness? And who can say, scientifically, that we might not be healthier and happier if this awareness was not dimmed by civilization? Dr. M. D. Coulter, who thinks that the esthetic sense could involve medicine, wrote in the *British Medical Journal*:

> Who would not even now stop in their tracks at the sound of the nightingale, or feast replete on the sparkle of the sun on the fresh moving sea? To cast these aside is to ignore the legacy of a thousand ages. . . . Why do so many people seem untouched by great music or the beauty of the natural world? Partly because it is for some not freely available and also because so often it is denied them at their most impressionable age.

The mass of people, living lives of work, hurry, preoccupation, and anxiety do not see nature's beauty. When they are

165

unhurried and at peace with themselves, the world can seem incredibly beautiful to ordinary people: the stars at night, the morning after a snowstorm, the flowers of spring. "I never see the dawn break or the sun set," wrote Emerson in his essay "Nature," "without reflecting 'what can be conceived so beautiful as actual nature?'"

A sense of beauty may be especially intense at moments of physical exhaustion or even of death. Lord Tweedsmuir (John Buchan) wrote of his experience in the Boer War that after a long trek following a late camp the night before ". . . though savagely hungry, I forgot about breakfast. Scents, sights, and sounds blended into a harmony so perfect that it transcended human expression, even human thought. . . . The world was a place of inexhaustible beauty. . . ." And speaking of a small company marching into a heavenly valley in Vietnam, the military historian S. L. A. Marshall wrote:

> What they saw made the war seem remote and their mission incongruous. Given only a few minutes to enjoy the setting as they marched, they made the most of their opportunity. The picture thereafter would remain with them imperishably, for such is the nature of man under pressure. While excitement holds, the individual may rise above his prior limits. Woodrow Wilson Sayre, writing of his fight against death on Mt. Everest, put it in this way: 'Surprisingly the sense of beauty is still sharp. How deep that sense must be within us. Even a man waiting to die will notice the loveliness of trees and sunlight around him.' I have found this to be true of much humbler men, combat hands who, unlike Sayre, did not possess an acute awareness of an unusual instance of order in art or nature.

I have read, in an account of one of Hitler's death camps, of the intense feeling of beauty that came to a girl dying of tuberculosis when she saw a spray of apple blossoms outside her barrack window. Why should extreme fatigue or approaching death make some otherwise indifferent people perceive the beauty of the world? Could it not be that the pressures and anxieties of civilization are lifted at these times? Recall the way highwaymen and pickpockets were said to look so peaceful when riding to the gallows, as though they had nothing more to worry about. "You cannot perceive beauty," wrote Thoreau, "but with a serene mind."

Among naturalists, none appear to have felt the sheer beauty of the world more than British author Richard Jefferies at the time his health was breaking up and he was about to die. At this time, as he wrote in *The Story of My Heart,*

> The familiar everyday scene was soon out of sight. I came to other trees, meadows and fields. I began to breathe a new air and to have a fresher aspiration. . . . By the blue heaven, by the rolling sun bursting through untrodden space, a new ocean of ether every day unveiled. By the fresh and wandering air encompassing the world, by the sea sounding on the shore—the green sea white-flecked at the margin and the deep ocean; by the strong earth under me.

I think it is because civilization imposes such heavy burdens that the best in us is often crushed. We do not think and feel as the great individuals we might be but only as members of the herd. How about scientists? Have they, by habits of precision and exactitude, risen above such things as the beauty of the world? Certainly not some of the abler ones. John Tyndall wrote of Faraday, one of the most honored scientists of all time:

> What to him was the splendor of a palace compared to a thunderstorm upon the Brighton Downs? What among all the appliances of royalty to compare with the setting sun? I refer to a thunderstorm and a sunset, because these things excited a kind of ecstasy in his mind, and to a mind open to such ecstasy the pomps and pleasures of the world are usually of small account. Nature, not education, rendered Faraday strong and refined.

Often when in the woods cutting trees and piling branches I

look up at the white clouds and blue sky, at the sun on the snow and white birches, and, exhilarated by the mountain air, I exclaim to myself, "Oh, beautiful world. Oh, wonderful day." Nature is not something to do with other men. It's something to get us away, at least for a time, from the turmoil of the world. The habit of watching birds and animals in beautiful places can, for a time, bring us closer to what we really are.

There are so many obstacles to our developing the sense of beauty. I wonder if too much preoccupation with intellectual matters does not kill the esthetic sense. Charles Darwin was exhilarated by beautiful scenery when younger but spoke of losing the pleasure he formerly took in it. Darwin, speculating on this phenomenon, wrote:

> My mind seems to have become a kind of machine for grinding general laws out of large collections of facts, but why this should have caused the atrophy of that part of the brain alone, on which the higher tastes depend, I cannot conceive. The loss of these tastes is a loss of happiness, and may possibly be injurious to the intellect, and more probably to the moral character, by enfeebling the emotional part of our nature.

Alexander Skutch, by far the greatest of living ornithologists, has retained his esthetic sense into old age. He writes of birds: "They charm us with lovely plumage and melodious song; our quest of them takes us to the fairest places; to find them and uncover their secrets, we exert ourselves greatly and live intensely." Frank Graham, Jr., who went to Costa Rica to interview Skutch, reports that "His attachment both to natural beauty and the extraordinary moments when the mind and senses savour it, is intense."

I feel sympathetic to Darwin's perception that loss of the esthetic sense is regrettable, but I think losing it is not inevitable with age but results from simple neglect. If a behavior watcher thinks about the beauty of the places where he goes to watch birds as well as the birds themselves, and if he keeps an eye out for both, he may retain the enthusiasm he had for both into old age. Enthusiasm for the beauty of life helps to keep the brain alive. And there is a practical aspect to it. Things do not always happen when one goes out to watch birds. There can be long stretches when nothing much seems to be going on, as when watching by the nest of a Pileated Woodpecker. At these times I switch to thinking how beautiful the world is, and instead of being impatient that the bird does not return, I find myself at peace with the world.

Man's love of animals and a desire to learn about them may also be innate. James Serpell, a research associate in animal behavior at Cambridge University, has shown, in his remarkable book *In the Company of Animals*, the depths of man's need for an exchange of affection and friendship. Contrary to the popular belief that only civilized man lavishes affection on animals, Serpell cites many examples of pets kept by primitive peoples. This leads him to the conclusion that "prehistoric man may have loved his dogs and his other domestic animals as pets long before he made use of them for any other purpose. Affection for pets may seem, in retrospect, trivial and unimportant. Yet it was probably indirectly responsible for one of the most profound and significant events in the history of our species." Serpell relates how in our time dogs, cats, and other animals have been used with remarkable success in therapy with lonely, withdrawn people in nursing homes and other places; but it is not only the incapacitated who may benefit. "Many pet-owners," writes Serpell, "claim that their animals have increased their circle of acquaintances and made them friends." Dogs, it has been noted, reflect the personality of their owners. "Thus the friendly dog is seen as an extension of a basically happy and friendly owner."

Sometimes I find a book by an amateur who, because he or she loves birds and animals, reaches an understanding of them well beyond what I encounter in most scientific texts. One such book is Barbara Woodhouse's *Talking with Animals*. As a young lady, the author went to an *estancia* or ranch in the Argentine pampas.

Forbidden to break in horses, she had a wild horse roped for her when the managers were away one day and, with words and kindness alone, had it tamed and was riding it alone three days later. When out riding, she met an Indian on a beautiful horse. After a few polite exchanges, she told him that she was taming the chestnut pony she was on. Woodhouse writes:

> He said he thought only his own tribe knew the secret of taming horses without fear, and, asked what it was, he told me to watch next time I turned strange horses out together and to see what they did. I asked what he meant, and he told me that horses always go up to each other and sniff each other's noses, which is their way of saying 'How do you do?' in their language, and that he always did the same when he wished to tame a horse himself. He said: 'Stand with your hands behind your back and blow gently down through your nostrils. Keep quite still, and the horse will come up to you and sniff and will blow up your own nose, after which all fear will have left him. That horse, providing that you don't give it reason to turn vicious, will always be your friend and the friend of man.'

The Indian's trick was a turning point in Barbara Woodhouse's life. She was soon promoted to breaking in all horses on the estancia at ten shillings apiece.

On returning to England, Woodhouse had remarkable success in dairy farming and then in training dogs. Although her interests were all in domestic animals, I think domestic animals make a good experience for anyone wanting to observe and get to know wild animals. As Woodhouse expresses it

> there is a language for every species of animal, bird, and reptile, if you study it long enough. . . . I feel that no matter what language is spoken, the same principles underlie everything. The talk, whatever its form, must be based on a great love, a great desire to be real friends with the animal, and, above all, complete freedom from fear. The love of animals and other creatures is a bond all human beings have with each other.

I know the truth of Barbara Woodhouse's words every time I go out to speak to my pet raven. It seems extraordinary to me that the approach, similar to Woodhouse's, that has made him such an affectionate and understanding bird should also work for a dog, a beaver, and other social mammals. No matter how many times professional behaviorists dismiss the notion as trivial, sentimental, or worst of all, "anthropomorphic," I still feel man is capable of bonds with other creatures because our instinctive, emotional lives have so much in common. "Believe me," wrote Konrad Lorenz in *King Solomon's Ring*, "I am not mistakenly assigning human properties to animals: on the contrary, I am showing you what an enormous animal inheritance remains in man to this day."

Speaking of the increasing dehumanization and depersonalization of man in his book *So Human an Animal*, René Dubos writes:

> In many respects, modern man is like a wild animal spending its life in a zoo; like the animal, he is fed abundantly and protected from inclemencies but deprived of natural stimuli essential for many functions of his body and mind. Man is alienated from nature, but more importantly from the deepest layers of his fundamental self.

What I like about behavior-watching, in the broad and inclusive sense I give to it, is that it not only strengthens my bonds with the beauty of nature, but also my empathy with living things. Goethe thought the worst thing that can happen to man is alienation from nature. Merging with nature for the time that one is absorbed in watching some bird or animal is a way of hanging onto the fundamental self that, in many people, seems in danger of extinction.

BIBLIOGRAPHY

GENERAL REFERENCES

Armstrong, Edward A. *Bird Display and Behavior*. New York: Dover Publications, Inc., 1965.

Terres, John K. *The Audubon Society Encyclopedia of North American Birds*. New York: Alfred A. Knopf, 1980.

Welty, Joel C. *The Life of Birds*. Philadelphia: W. B. Saunders Company, 1975.

PREVIOUS BOOKS BY THE AUTHOR

Kilham, Lawrence. *Never Enough of Nature*. Foster, Rhode Island: Droll Yankees, Inc., 1977. (Republished under the title *A Naturalist's Field Guide*. Harrisburg, Pennsylvannia: Stackpole Bros., 1981.)

————. "Life history studies of woodpeckers of Eastern North America." *Nuttall Ornithological Club*, Publication No. 20 (1983): 1–240.

————. *The American Crow and the Common Raven*. College Station, Texas: Texas A & M University Press, scheduled to appear in January, 1989.

PREFACE

Griffin, Donald R. *Animal Thinking*. Cambridge: Harvard University Press, 1984.

Leo, J. "All that jizz." *Time* (May 25, 1987): 70–75.

Wilson, Edward O. "Karl von Frisch and the magic well." *Science* 159 (1968): 864–865.

CHAPTER 1

Beston, H. *The Outermost House*. New York: Doubleday, Doran and Co., Inc., 1933.

Chapman, Frank R. *Handbook to Birds of Eastern North America.* New York: D. Appleton and Co., 1924.

Forbush, Edward Howe. *Birds of Massachusetts and Other New England States.* Vols. 1–3. Boston: Commonwealth of Massachusetts, 1925–1929.

Kilham, Lawrence. "Snapping turtle in February." *Copeia* 170 (1929): 56.

———. "The abundance of English winter birds." *Audubon Magazine* 45 (1943): 304–305.

———. "European bird experiences. Germany and Austria." *Bulletin of the Massachusetts Audubon Society* 31 (1947): 3–8.

Townsend, Charles W. *Beach Grass.* Boston: Marshall Jones Co., 1923.

Zinsser, Hans. *Rats, Lice and History.* Boston: Little, Brown and Company, 1935.

CHAPTER 2

Bent, A. C. "Life histories of North American thrushes, kinglets and their allies." *U. S. National Museum Bulletin* 196 (1949): 344–345.

Brewster, William. "The birds of Lake Umbagog region of Maine." *Bulletin of the Museum of Comparative Zoology* 66 (Part 2) (1925): 375–376.

———. *Concord River.* Cambridge: Harvard University Press, 1937.

Errington, Paul L. *On Predation and Life.* Ames, Iowa: Iowa State University Press, 1967.

Fleming, R. C. "Possibly altruistic behavior in a White-breasted Nuthatch." *Jack-pine Warbler* 57 (1979): 217.

Kilham, Lawrence. "Actions of Worm-eating Warbler in defense of young." *Atlantic Naturalist* 8 (1952): 35.

———. "Courtship behavior of the Pied-billed Grebe." *Wilson Bulletin* 66 (1954): 65.

———. "Repeated territorial attacks of Pied-billed Grebe on Ring-necked Duck." *Wilson Bulletin* 66 (1954): 265–267.

————. "Breeding and other habits of Casqued Hornbills (*By-canistes subcylindricus*)." *Smithsonian Miscellaneous Collection* 131(9) (1956): vi + 1–45.

————. "Territorial behavior in Pikas." *Journal of Mammalogy* 39 (1958): 307.

————. "Eating of sand by Blue Jays." *Condor* 62 (1960): 295–296.

————. "Reproductive behavior of White-breasted Nuthatches. 1. Distraction display, bill-sweeping and nest hole defense." *Auk* 85 (1968): 175–176.

————. "Use of blister beetle in bill-sweeping by White-breasted Nuthatch." *Auk* 88 (1971): 175–176.

————. "Caterwauling of the Barred Owl: a speculation." *New Hampshire Audubon Quarterly* 25 (1972): 93–94.

————. "Reaction of birds to injured conspecifics." *Jack-pine Warbler* 59 (1981): 67–68.

CHAPTER 3

Kilham, Lawrence. "Pair formation, mutual tapping and nest hole selection of Red-bellied Woodpeckers." *Auk* 75 (1958): 318–329.

————. "Sealed-in winter stores of Red-headed Woodpeckers." *Wilson Bulletin* 70 (1958): 107–113.

————. "Territorial behavior in wintering Red-headed Woodpeckers." *Wilson Bulletin* 70 (1959): 347–358.

————. "Mutual tapping of the Red-headed Woodpecker." *Auk* 76 (1959): 235–236.

————. "Feeding behavior of Downy Woodpeckers. 1. Preference for paper birches and sexual differences." *Auk* 87 (1965): 544–556.

————. "Reproductive behavior of Hairy Woodpeckers. 1. Pair formation and courtship." *Auk* 78 (1966): 251–265.

————. "Life history studies of the woodpeckers of eastern North America." *Nuttall Ornithological Club*, Publication No. 20 (1983): 1–240.

————. "Pileated pairing." *Birder's World* 1 (1987): 6–8.

Lack, David. *The Life of the Robin*. London: H. F. & G. Witherby, Ltd., 1943.

Nice, M. M. "Studies in the life history of the Song Sparrow. 1. A population study of the Song Sparrow." *Transactions of the Linnaean Society of New York* 4 (1937): 1–247.

————. "Studies in the life history of the Song Sparrow." *Transactions of the Linnaean Society of New York* 6 (1943): 1–328.

————. *Research Is a Passion with Me*. Toronto: Consolidated Amethyst Communications, Inc., 1979.

Summers–Smith, D. *The House Sparrow*. London: Collins, 1963.

CHAPTER 4

Burgess, Thornton W. *Now I Remember*. Boston: Little, Brown and Company, 1960.

Corbo, M. S. and D. M. Barras. *Arnie the Darling Starling*. Boston: Houghton Mifflin Company, 1983.

Darwin, F. (ed.). *Autobiography of Charles Darwin*. London: Watts & Co., 1929.

Davis, E. R. "Friendly siskins." *Bird Lore* 27 (1926): 381–388.

Griffin, Donald R. *Animal Thinking*. Cambridge: Harvard University Press, 1984.

Howard, Len. *Birds as Individuals*. London: Collins, 1952.

Kipps, Clare. *Clarence: The Life of a Sparrow*. New York: G. P. Putnam, 1954.

Sherman, Althea R. 1952. *Birds of an Iowa Dooryard*. Boston: The Christopher Publishing House, 1952.

CHAPTER 5

Francis, A. M. "Wing- and tail-flappings of Anhingas: a possible method of drying in the absence of sun." *Auk* 98 (1981): 834.

Kilham, Lawrence. "Alarm call of Crested Guan when attacked by Ornate Hawk-Eagle." *Condor* 80 (1978): 347–348.

————. "Snake and pond snails as food of Gray-necked Wood-Rails." *Condor* 81 (1979): 100–101.

————. "Courtship of Common Caracaras in Costa Rica." *Raptor Research* 13 (1979): 17–19.

CHAPTER 6

Chapman, Frank M. *Camps and Cruises of an Ornithologist*. New York: D. Appleton and Co., 1908.

Kilham, Lawrence. "Cocked-tail display and evasive behavior of American Oystercatcher." *Auk* 97 (1980): 205.

————. "Courtship feeding and copulation of Royal Terns." *Wilson Bulletin* 93 (1981): 390–391.

Matthiessen, Peter. *The Wind Birds*. New York: Viking Press, 1973.

Ternes, A. P. "Picnic a la dauphine." Summarized in *Natural History* 95 (1986): 70–73.

CHAPTER 7

Brandt, T. H. *Alaska Bird Trails*. Cleveland: Bird Research Foundation, 1943.

Kilham, Lawrence. "Pre-nesting behavior of the Swallow-tailed Kite (*Elanoides forficatus*), including interference by an un-mated male with a breeding pair." *Raptor Research* 14 (1980): 29–31.

————. "Association of Great Egret and White Ibis." *Journal of Field Ornithology* 51 (1980): 73–74.

————. "Assemblages of Tree Swallows as information centers." *Florida Field Naturalist* 8 (1980): 26–28.

————. "Red-shouldred Hawks whirling with talons locked in conflict." *Raptor Research* 15 (1981): 123–124.

————. "Alligator with young threatens Great Blue Heron." *Florida Field Naturalist* 13 (1985): 68–70.

Snyder, N. F. R. "Breeding biology of Swallow-tailed Kites in Florida." *Living Bird* 13 (1974): 73–97.

Stone, W. *Bird Studies at Old Cape May*. New York: Dover Publications, Inc., 1965.

Ward, Peter and A. Zahavi. "The importance of certain assemblages of birds as 'information centers' for food finding." *Ibis* 115 (1973): 517–534.

CHAPTER 8

Evans, M. A. and H. E. Evans. "Ants, elephants, and men." *American Scientist* 54 (1966): 110–118.

Lawick–Goodall, J. van. *My Friends the Wild Chimpanzees*. Washington, D. C.: National Geographic Society, 1967.

Maurois, André. *The Life of Alexander Fleming*. New York: E. P. Dutton & Co., Inc., 1959.

Nicolle, Charles. *Biologie de l'Invention*. Paris: F. Alcan, 1932.

Sandburg, Carl. *Abraham Lincoln: The Prairie Years*. New York: Harcourt, Brace & Co., 1926.

Yoeli, Meir. "Charles Nicolle and the frontiers of medicine." *New England Journal of Medicine* 276 (1967): 670–675.

Zinsser, Hans. *As I Remember Him*. Boston: Little, Brown and Co., 1940.

CHAPTER 9

Avery, M. L. "Diet and breeding seasonality among a population of Sharp-tailed Monias, *Lonchura striata*, in Malaysia." *Auk* 97 (1980): 160–166.

Bent, A. C. "Life histories of North American nuthatches, wrens, thrashers and their allies." *U. S. National Museum Bulletin* 195 (1948): 2.

Digioia, H. G. "American Goldfinches eating algae." *Oriole* 39 (1974): 47.

Howard, H. E. *Territory in Bird Life*. London: John Murray, 1920.

Kilham, Lawrence. "Territorial behavior of red squirrel." *Journal of Mammalogy* 35 (1954): 252–253.

————. "Egg-carrying by the Whip-poor-will." *Wilson Bulletin* 69 (1957): 113–114.

————. "Tree den of fisher." *New Hampshire Audubon Quarterly.* 28 (1970): 13–15.

————. "Roosting habits of White-breasted Nuthatches." *Condor* 73 (1971): 113–114.

————. "Reproductive behavior of White-breasted Nuthatches. 11. Courtship." *Auk* 89 (1972): 115–129.

————. "Goldfinches feeding on filamentous algae." *Oriole* 45 (1982): 48.

CHAPTER 10

Buyukmichi, H. S. *Hour of the Beaver.* New York: Rand McNally and Co., 1971.

Eastman, C. A. *Indian Boyhood.* New York: Dover Publications, Inc., 1971.

Mech, David. "At home with the arctic wolf." *National Geographic* 171 (1987): 562–593.

Miles, Hugh. *The Track of the Wild Otter.* London: Elm Tree Books / Hamish, Hamilton, Ltd. 1984.

Owens, Mark and Delia. *Cry of the Kalahari.* Boston: Houghton Mifflin Co., 1984.

Richards, Dorothy. *Beaversprite.* San Francisco: Chronicle Books, 1977.

Rue, L. L. *The World of the Beaver.* New York: J. B. Lippincott Co., 1964.

Wilsson, Lars. *My Beaver Colony.* Garden City: Doubleday & Co., 1968.

CHAPTER 11

Kilham, Lawrence. "Biology of young Belted Kingfishers." *American Midland Naturalist* 92 (1974): 245–247.

Lindbergh, A. M. *Gift of the Sea.* New York: Pantheon Books, Inc., 1955.

CHAPTER 12

Buchan, John (Lord Tweedsmuir). *Pilgrim's Way*. Boston: Houghton Miflin Co., 1940.

Coulter, M. D. "Personal view." *British Medical Journal* 3 (1973): 345.

Darwin, F. (ed.) *Autobiography of Charles Darwin*. London: Watts & Co., 1929.

Dubos, René, *So Human an Animal*. New York: Charles Scribner's Sons, 1968.

Graham, F., Jr. "Alexander Skutch and the appreciative mind." *Audubon Magazine* (March, 1974): 83–117.

Jeffries, Richard. *The Story of My Heart*. New York: Macmillan / St. Martin's Press, 1968.

Lorenz, Konrad. *King Solomon's Ring*. New York: Thomas Y. Crowel Co., 1952.

Marshall, S. L. A. *Battles in the Monsoon*. Nashville, Tennessee: Battery Press, 1966.

Serpell, James. *In the Company of Animals*. Oxford: Basil Blackwell, 1986.

Tyndall, John. *Faraday as a Discoverer*. New York: Thomas Y. Crowell Company, 1961.

Woodhouse, Barbara. *Talking to Animals*. New York: Stein & Day, 1970.

LIST OF COMMON AND SCIENTIFIC NAMES

Alligator, *Alligator mississippiensis*
Anhinga, *Anhinga anhinga*
Anole, Green, *Anolis carolinensis*
Beaver, *Castor canadensis*
Beetle, Whirligig, *Gyrinus* species
Blackbird, European, *Turdus merula*
Blackbird, Melodious, *Dives dives*
Caracara, Common, *Caracara cheriway*
Catbird, Gray, *Dumetella carolinensis*
Chickadee, Black-capped, *Parus atricapillus*
Chickadee, Carolina, *Parus carolinensis*
Coot, American, *Fulica americana*
Cormorant, *Phalocrocorax auritus*
Crab, Fiddler, *Uca pugnax*
Crane, Crowned, *Balearica pavonina*
Crane, Sandhill, *Grus canadensis*
Creeper, Brown, *Certhia familiaris*
Crocodile, Nile, *Crocodilus nioloticus*
Crow, American, *Corvus brachyrhynchos*
Curlew, Stone, *Burhinus oedicnemus*
Deer, *Odocoileus virginianus*
Dolphin, Bottle-nosed, *Tursiops truncatus*
Duck, Black-bellied Tree-, *Dendrocygna autumnalis*
Duck, Ring-necked, *Aythya collaris*
Eagle, Short-toed, *Circaetus gallicus*
Egret, Cattle, *Bubulcus ibis*
Egret, Great, *Casmerodious albus*
Egret, Snowy, *Leucophoyx thula*
Fairy, Purple-crowned, *Heliothrix barroti*
Falcon, Orange-breasted, *Falco deiroleucus*

Fisher, *Martes pennanti*
Flicker, Common, *Colaptes auratus*
Frog, Green, *Rana clamitans*
Frog, Pickerel, *Rana palustris*
Gallinule, Common, *Gallinula chloropus*
Goldfinch, American, *Carduelis tristis*
Gnatcatcher, Blue-gray, *Polioptila caerulea*
Grackle, Common, *Quiscalus quiscula*
Grebe, Pied-billed, *Podilymbus podiceps*
Guan, Crested, *Penelope purpurascens*
Harrier, Hen, *Circus cyaneus* (Europe)
Harrier, Marsh, *Circus aeruginosus* (Europe)
Harrier, Marsh, *Circus cyaneus*
Harrier, Montagu's, *Circus pygargus*
Hawk, Red-shouldered, *Buteo lineatus*
Hawk-Eagle, Ornate, *Spizaetus ornatus*
Heron, Bare-throated Tiger-, *Tigrisoma mexicanum*
Heron, Boat-billed, *Cochlearius cochlearius*
Heron, Great Blue, *Ardea herodias*
Heron, Green, *Butorides striatus*
Heron, Little Blue, *Egretta caerula*
Heron, Tricolored, *Hydramassa tricolor*
Hornbill, Casqued, *Bycamistes subcylindricus*
Ibis, White, *Eudocimus albus*
Iguana, *Iguana iguana*
Jacana, *Jacana soinosa*
Jay, Blue, *Cyanocitta cristata*
Kestrel, American, *Falco sparverius*
Killdeer, *Charadrius vociferus*
Kingbird, Eastern, *Tyrannus tyrannus*
Kingfisher, Belted, *Megaceryle alcyon*
Kinglet, Golden-crowned, *Regulus satrapa*
Kite, *Milvus milvus*
Kite, Swallow-tailed, *Elanoides forficatus*
Lapwing, *Vanellus vanellus*
Limpkin, *Aramus guarauna*

Mink, *Mustela vison*
Mockingbird, Northern, *Mimus polyglottos*
Monkey, Howler, *Alonatta palleata*
Muskrat, *Odontra zibetheca*
Newt, Red-spotted, *Notophthalmus viridescens*
Nightjar, Freckled, *Caprimulgus tristigma*
Nuthatch, Red-breasted, *Sitta canadensis*
Nuthatch, White-breasted, *Sitta carolinensis*
Otter, River, *Lutra canadensis*
Owl, Barred, *Strix varia*
Owl, Ferruginous Pygmy-, *Glaucidium brasilianum*
Owl, Great Horned, *Bubo virginianus*
Owl, Screech, *Otus asio*
Oystercatcher, American, *Haematopus palliatus*
Parrakeet, Orange-fronted, *Aratinga camcularis*
Peccary, Collared, *Dicotyles tajacu*
Peccary, White-lipped, *Tayassu albirostris*
Pelican, Brown, *Pelecanus occidentalis*
Peregrine, *Falco peregrinus*
Phoebe, Eastern, *Sayornis phoebe*
Pika, *Ochotona princeps*
Porcupine, *Erithizon dorsatum*
Porcupine, Prehensile-tailed, *Coendo prehensilis*
Quealea, Red-billed, *Quelea quelea*
Racer, Black, *Coluber constrictor*
Raven, *Corvus corax*
Robin, American, *Turdus migratorius*
Robin, European, *Erithacus rubecula*
Sandpiper, Buff-breasted, *Tryngites subruficollis*
Sandpiper, Spotted, *Actitis macularia*
Sapsucker, Yellow-bellied, *Sphyrapicus varius*
Shrew, Water, *Sorex palustris*
Siskin, Pine, *Spinus pinus*
Skunk, Common Striped, *Mephitis mephitis*
Sparrow, House, *Passer domesticus*
Sparrow, Song, *Melospiza melodia*

Squirrel, Gray, *Sciurus carolinensis*
Squirrel, Red, *Sciurus canadensis*
Starling, *Sturnus vulgaris*
Swallow, Tree, *Iridoprocne bicolor*
Swift, Chimney, *Chaetura pelagica*
Teal, Blue-winged, *Anas discors*
Tern, Caspian, *Hydroprogne caspia*
Tern, Royal, *Sterna maxima*
Tinamou, Great, *Tinamus major*
Tit, Blue, *Parus caeruleus*
Titmouse, Tufted, *Parus bicolor*
Toad, *Bufo americanus*
Turkey, Wild, *Meleagris galloparvo*
Turtle, Snapping, *Chelydra serpentina*
Vulture, Turkey, *Cathartes aura*
Warbler, Magnolia, *Dendroica magnolia*
Waterthrush, Northern, *Seiurus noveboracensis*
Weasel, Long-tailed, *Mustela frenata*
Whimbrel, *Numenius phaeopus*
Willet, *Catoptrophorus semipalmatus*
Woodcock, American, *Philohela minor*
Woodpecker, Black, *Dryocopus martius*
Woodpecker, Crimson-crested, *Campephilus melanoleucos*
Woodpecker, Downy, *Picoides pubescens*
Woodpecker, Hairy, *Picoides villosus*
Woodpecker, Hoffman's, *Melanerpes hoffmannii*
Woodpecker, Lineated, *Dryocopus lineatus*
Woodpecker, Pileated, *Dryocopus pileatus*
Woodpecker, Red-bellied, *Melanerpes carolinus*
Woodpecker, Red-cockaded, *Picoides borealis*
Woodpecker, Red-headed, *Melanerpes erythrocephalus*
Wood-Rail, Gray-necked, *Aramides cajanea*
Wren, House, *Troglodytes aedon*
Yellow-throat, Northern, *Geothlypis trichas*

INDEX

185

On Watching Birds was designed by Ann Aspell. It was typeset in Garamond by Dartmouth Printing Company. It was printed on Warren's Sebago, an acid-free paper, by Halliday Lithograph.